Dear David:

Our sages tell us that he who doesn't increase his knowledge, decreases it. Since knowledge is power use it wisely. Read this volume and broaden your understanding of your people's great Torah. Good luck on this your Bar Mitzvah day.

Mr Mrs Max Epstein

1949

THE STORY OF
BIBLE TRANSLATIONS

THE STORY OF
BIBLE TRANSLATIONS

BY

MAX L. MARGOLIS

PHILADELPHIA
THE JEWISH PUBLICATION SOCIETY OF AMERICA
5708-1948

60

PRINTED IN THE UNITED STATES OF AMERICA
PRESS OF THE JEWISH PUBLICATION SOCIETY
PHILADELPHIA, PENNA.

TO

PHILIP N. AND CARRIE G. ARONSON

IN FILIAL LOVE

CONTENTS

ILLUSTRATIONS

(Size Reduced)

CHAPTER I

THE TARGUM

It is not my intention in these pages to add one more reference-work to the many excellent ones which have to do with Bible translations. Bibliographical completeness will not be attempted. I shall

Prefatory Remarks. confine myself to the Hebrew Scriptures of which alone I may speak with first-hand knowledge, but even so the subject is a vast one. The external or human side must needs receive attention, but the general reader will none the less be interested to learn how the epoch-making translations go with great cultural and religious upheavals and how all of them display certain characteristics which seem to inhere in the oldest and youngest alike.

The Object of Bible Translation. The Torah which Israel received with joyful readiness at the foot of mount Sinai was in the opinion of the rabbis originally intended for all mankind as a guide to their salvation. God spoke not in secret (Isaiah 45. 19), but in the open and free desert, that all men might have access to the revealed Word; indeed the Torah was offered first to the Gentiles, but

Esau and Ishmael and other nations were unwilling to forego killing and immorality and stealing which the Decalogue forbids. The rabbis also assert that Joshua had the Torah engraved upon the stones of the altar (Joshua 8. 30-32) not only in the original, but also in all the other tongues of the world. Of these translations the nations secured transcripts, but after reading them, they turned their back upon the Torah. Accordingly, the object of the translation would have been to make the Scriptures known to the alien. There is an element of truth in this contention, and we shall come to speak of it in connection with the earliest Greek translation (chapter II). It may suffice for the present to recall the recognition conceded by Maimonides to the two daughter-religions that through them the words of the Torah have been spread to the utmost isles and among many nations. The great Jewish thinker would have accorded unstinted praise to the stupendous efforts of modern Bible societies (chapter VII). Yet for all that the primary object of Bible translation was to serve a need nearer home, that those to whom the original was a sealed book might profit by reading the Scriptures in the language spoken by them.

Just at what time among the Jews of Palestine Hebrew ceased to be the spoken language of the people is a mooted question. The older view has it that the Jews lost their Hebrew speech in the Baby-

The Change of Speech in Palestine. lonian captivity whence they brought back with them the Aramaic. Hebrew and Aramaic are sister languages be-longing to the group known as Semitic and comprising in addition Arabic, Ethiopic, and Assyro-Babylonian. There is a close resemblance among them all in structure and vocabulary, and Hebrew is related to Aramaic as Low German or Dutch is to High German. The people, of course, have no ear for resemblances often disguised, plain though they may be to the scholar. In the days of Hezekiah Aramaic was understood by the courtiers; to the common soldier it meant an unintelligible gib-berish. Ezra (in the fifth century) is reported to have read the Law to the assembled people 'dis-tinctly' (Nehemiah 8. 8); according to the rabbis, he read 'with interpretation,' that is, with an accom-panying rendition into the Aramaic. That, of course, may simply imply the carrying of a custom in vogue at a later period back to Ezra, to whom many other institutions are ascribed. It has been urged that the Aramaic spoken in Palestine was a dialect differing from the Babylonian variety and could not have been imported from the East. It has therefore been

2

argued that the change of speech must have occurred
in Palestine itself a century or so after Ezra.   But
we know now that the Jewish military colony, which
settled in Egypt long before Cambyses (529-522),
spoke and wrote Aramaic in the days of Nehemiah.
We must understand that the change in Palestine was
gradual, Hebrew succumbing in the North earlier
than in the South.   For a time indeed both languages
were spoken and understood, until at length Hebrew
vanished from the mouth of the people.   As late as
the second century of the current era Hebrew was
still spoken in some nook or corner, but in the main it
had become a sacred tongue understood by the
learned, but unknown to the unlettered who con-
versed in Aramaic.

But the Word of God was to be understood of the
people.   Just how early the custom arose for the
Scriptures, the Torah and the Prophets in particular,

The Oral Targum.   to be read on the sabbath in the synagogue
is not known.   But when these lessons had
become a fixed institution, it followed of
necessity that a translation into the people's speech
should go hand in hand with the reading of the original.   The rabbis call all translations Targum, but the
name is specifically applied to the Aramaic version.
At first the Targum was oral.   Beside the reader

stood the Targeman (hence the word 'dragoman'), the official interpreter. A verse, or in the case of the Prophets a connected section not exceeding three verses, was read in the Hebrew and immediately translated into Aramaic. Both the original, from the scroll, and the translation, from memory, were to be declaimed in the same pitch, and the interpreter was enjoined not to lean against the desk, but in deferential posture to stand some way off. The translation frequently assumed the character of free exposition with a view to inculcating the interpretation which the schools placed upon a law or custom and in general to bringing down the scriptural word to the comprehension of the common people. The prophetic lessons naturally lent themselves to amplification; the interpreter turned preacher, prefacing his remarks with a direct address to the congregation in some such words as 'O my people, sons of Israel,' or 'The prophet saith.' This freedom had its dangers, especially at the time of the rise of the heresies out of which a new religion was born. The Talmud discountenances the practice of certain interpreters who introduce the law Leviticus 22. 28 ('whether it be cow or ewe, ye shall not kill it and its young both in one day') with the homily: 'As our Father is merciful in Heaven, so shall ye be merciful on earth.' The rabbis themselves enjoin the imitation of divine mercy: ' As He is gracious and merciful, so be thou gracious and merciful.'   Nevertheless the plea is made that the commandments of the Torah must not be turned into mere ethical prescriptions.   The translator must not wander too far from the original. ' He who renders a verse as it reads, with strict literalness, lies; he that makes additions is a blasphemer.'   In Leviticus 18. 21 it is forbidden to give over of one's seed unto Molech; the Mishnah makes mention of a paraphrastic (free) rendering by which the prohibition was made to refer to sacrificing one's offspring through intercourse with a pagan woman.   The abominable Molech worship had become a thing forgotten, and the translators thought themselves justified in applying the scriptural condemnation to a regrettable laxity prevalent in their days.   Nevertheless such translators were to be silenced with rebuke. The wording of the original was paramount, and a translator who made the slightest error by investing a Hebrew word with an unwonted meaning was publicly corrected.   Among the instances cited are the renderings ' (plain) herbs ' for ' bitter herbs ' (Exodus 12. 8) and ' vessel ' for ' basket ' (Deuteronomy 26. 2).   To quote a parallel from another quarter: when the book of Jonah was read in a Christian church in Africa from Jerome's new Latin version (chapter III), there was an uproar, because

the miraculous plant (4. 6), which in the older translation based upon the Greek had been rendered
' gourd,' was now identified with the ' ivy.'

The rabbis looked with disfavor upon written
Targums. Translation naturally partook of the
character of interpretation, and all interpretation
Rabbinic was classed with the oral law. It was
Disapproval believed that when Moses delivered the
of Written written Law into the keeping of the
Targums. priests he also instructed his successor
Joshua, and Joshua the elders, and the
elders the prophets, and the prophets the men of the
Great Synagogue, in all the ramifications of each
subject by word of mouth. Writing seemed to
bestow a measure of sacredness, and nothing was to
rival the Scriptures in authority. ' Only the things
written might be written; what was handed down by
word of mouth must be transmitted orally.' The
written Word of God, moreover, was held to be
capable of more than one sense; to fasten upon it just
one was not permissible. However, it was not so
much the written copy that was placed under the
ban as the public use of it. Written Targums were
found in private possession at an early time. Rabbi
Samuel son of Isaac (in the fourth century), on
entering the synagogue, remonstrated with a scribe
who read from a written Targum. At an earlier

period it is reported of Gamaliel the Elder that he had a copy of the Targum of the book of Job immured beneath a layer of stones in the Temple. When a fire broke out on the sabbath, such volumes, as indeed copies of any other translation of the Scriptures, were to be saved along with the scrolls of the original; but the former must then be stored away, withdrawn from public use. The ancients had a wonderful memory, but as the traditional lore grew in magnitude and the retentiveness of scholars weakened, the private volumes were produced and successively recast, until at length they became the public property of the Jewish people. Mishnah, Gemara, Targum, all passed through similar stages of growth, each with its Palestinian recension and its Babylonian counterpart. Just as the Babylonian Talmud supplanted the Palestinian in point of authority, so the Babylonian Targums overshadowed those of Palestine out of which they had grown, the Babylonian schools placing their seal of approval upon a form suitable to the needs of the time.

Targum Onkelos. In the foremost rank stands the Babylonian Targum of the Pentateuch which goes by the name of Onkelos. When in the sequel Aramaic had given place to Arabic as the language spoken by Eastern Jewry, or when in the West the Jews had adopted the speech of the European

BRITISH MUSEUM — ABOUT 1300 C. E.

With the Targum after each verse and Masoretic notes in the margins nations, this Targum continued to be read and studied. On the eve of the sabbath it was customary to read the lesson in advance, twice in the original and once in the Targum. The wording of the translation was as zealously guarded as that of the original. According to the Babylonian Talmud, the version was the work of Onkelos the proselyte under the supervision of Rabbi Eliezer and Rabbi Joshua; but the statement, it has been clearly shown, rests upon a misunderstanding: the parallel statement in the Palestinian Talmud speaks of Aquila (Akylas) who translated the Scriptures into Greek (chapter II). Internal evidence points to the times of Rabbi Akiba in which the earlier layers of the Targum must be sought. Thus the language is but slightly tinged with foreign elements, and those are mainly Greek; where the parallel Targums of Palestinian redaction (see below) make mention of Byzantium or Constantinople, Onkelos speaks of the Romans; where Onkelos indulges in amplification of a legal (halakic) or sermonic (haggadic) character, he reproduces matter taught by Akiba and his school. The homeland of the Targum was certainly Palestine: the Aramaic of its diction is unmistakably of the Western variety, but slightly retouched by Babylonian or Eastern idioms. It was in Babylonia, however, that the Targum became authoritative in home and school.

To the scholars of the Babylonian Talmud this Targum is 'our Targum,' the one in general currency and universally recognized, as opposed to the rendering of this or that scholar operating in his own personal capacity. 'As we translate' is a frequently recurrent mode of citing it. In particular it was Rab Joseph the Blind (died in the year 323) who was familiar with the Targum, although other scholars before and after him quote from it. In the main the Targum ascribed to Onkelos exhibits a marked fidelity to the wording of the original, yet not at the cost of intelligibility; only here and there the literal rendering is given up so as to inculcate a legal point, and in the poetic passages the text is somewhat freely expanded with a view to weaving in a homily of the rabbis. It is certainly free from all the spurious renderings of the kind referred to above, which the rabbis discountenanced. The production apparently was suffered to reach the people only after it had passed muster under the critical eye of the responsible leaders. It is indeed a learned piece of work. It was meant to supersede the ampler and more popular versions upon which it probably rests. In revising the older models the author proved rather editor, excising any feature that seemed objectionable. He gave to the people that which in his opinion they most stood in need of and in a manner suitable to their comprehension.

It is fortunate, however, that the other Targums
to which authority was denied did not wholly perish.
We have for the Pentateuch a parallel Aramaic translation which is spoken of as the Targum of Jerusalem
The or the Palestinian. It used to go erro-
Palestinian neously by the name of Targum Jona-
Editions. than; it is therefore frequently referred
to as Pseudo-Jonathan. Side by side
with the complete text runs a parallel recension
extant in a fragmentary condition. In point of
redaction this Targum is certainly posterior to Onkelos; in Genesis 21. 21 the names given to Ishmael's
wives are apparently those of Mohammed's. On the
other hand, elements of high antiquity are not wanting, as when in Deuteronomy 33. 11 we read: ' The
enemies of the high priest Johanan shall not survive.'
Moreover, it has preserved traces of an older norm
of law (halakah), and points to many variations
from the received Hebrew text. In general, the
Palestinian Targum embellishes the text with sermonic (haggadic) expansions; in it are also found
objectionable renderings castigated by the rabbis.

Our Targum of the Prophets was, like that
of Onkelos, edited in Babylonia, but we possess
scanty remains of a Palestinian recension. According to the passage in the Babylonian Talmud which
ascribes the Pentateuch Targum to Onkelos, the

author of the translation of the Prophets was a disciple of Hillel by the name of Jonathan son of
Uzziel. The Babylonian teachers (Amoraim) were
well acquainted with it, and here again Rab Joseph

The Targums for the other Parts of the Scriptures. is responsible for most of the cita-
tions. It naturally contains both
older and more recent matter, but it
is free from polemics with Christianity. In the Latter Prophets (Isaiah–
Malachi) the subject-matter lent itself to paraphrastic embellishment, while in the historical books
(Joshua–Kings) there is on the whole a scrupu-
lous adherence to the letter. The Targums to the
third section of the Scriptures (the Writings, Ketubim : Psalms–Chronicles) are peculiar to the Palestin-
ians. They never appear to have received official
sanction. Some, like those on the Song of Songs,
Ecclesiastes, and one of the three on Esther, partake
of the nature of midrashic works, while others, like
the translation of the Psalter (contrast, however, the
lengthy homily to Psalm 91), are literalistic. The
Targum of Proverbs seems to have been taken over
from the Christian Syrians (chapter III), as is shown
by the language and the points of contact with the
Septuagint. In all of them old material stands side
by side with later elements, as when in Psalm 83. 7
the Hungarians are mentioned. The Samaritans,

likewise, possess an Aramaic translation, naturally confined to the Pentateuch which alone they recognize as Scripture.

The chief importance which attaches to the Aramaic Targum lies in the fact that it enables us to gain an insight into the interpretation of the Scriptures at a time when tradition had not yet wholly died out. Not only those Targums which received official sanction, but also those less authoritative, keep close to the sentiments of the Synagogue, and constitute an invaluable source of information concerning the religious development in post-biblical times. Naturally the ideas which run through the Targum are identical with those which the talmudic-midrashic literature opens up to us; moreover, they have their points of contact with an older period in which the later writings of the biblical collection itself had their origin. When Maimonides engaged in warfare upon the notion which ascribed bodily form to the Deity, he was able to point to the authority of the Targums, of Onkelos in particular. The scholars may full-well know that the prophets indulge in similes likening the Creator to the creature and that the scriptural modes of speech are merely accommodations to the human ear; not so the ordinary folk. For their

Character of the Targum.

Anthropomorphisms toned down.

sake the human traits attributed to the Deity are sedulously toned down. Thus God does not smell the sweet savor of an offering, but accepts it with pleasure; on the Passover night He does not pass over the Israelites, but spares them; He does not go before the people, He leads it; instead of God hearing or seeing, it is said that it was heard or revealed before Him; the hand that covers Moses becomes the protecting Word, just as the wind which He blows is the Word which He speaks; the finger of God is reduced to a blow from before Him, God's feet are His glorious throne, and God's staff is the staff wherewith miracles are wrought. Actions unbecoming God, as when He meets Moses to slay him (Exodus 4. 24), are ascribed to His angel. Just as God must not be humanized, divine appellations may not be used of human beings. Moses is to be to Aaron a master, not a God. The sons of God who took the daughters of man for wives were not even angels, for angels do not go a-wooing, but sons of rulers. There cannot be any comparison between the Lord and the gods. ' Who is like unto Thee among the gods? who is like Thee, etc.' (Exodus 15. 11) is made to read: ' There is none beside Thee, for Thou art God, O Lord; there is none except Thyself.' All personification of inanimate objects is wiped out. The promised land does not flow with milk and honey, but yields those products; the sword does not come, but murderers with the sword; Ezekiel does not eat the scroll, but listens attentively to its contents; and the proverb: ' The fathers have eaten sour grapes, and the children's teeth are set on edge ' is paraphrased into the statement that the fathers have sinned and the children are beaten. Thus in deference to the ordinary intelligence which may take a figure of speech literally all the poetry of the original is sacrificed, and the elevated style of the sacred writers is reduced to com-

The Honor of the Jewish People guarded. monplace. Where the honor of the Jewish people or of the heroes of biblical times is involved pains are taken that nothing of a derogatory character may adhere to them. Israel is not ' a perverse and crooked generation,' nor ' a foolish people and unwise,' but ' a generation that hath changed its deeds and is become changed, and a people that received the Law and learned not wisdom.' Rachel does not steal her father's household gods, she merely takes them; Jacob does not steal Laban's heart, as the Hebrew idiom has it, he just hides from him his departure; indeed he departs, he does not flee; nor does Israel flee from Egypt, he departs. Moses does not marry a Cushite woman, but a beautiful woman; Leah's eyes were pretty, not weak. An extreme case occurs in Genesis 49. 14 f., where the sense of the original is turned into its very opposite. Instead of becoming a servant under taskwork, Issachar, according to the rendering of Onkelos, shall conquer the provinces of nations and destroy their inhabitants, levying tribute upon them that are left over.

An Ancient Tendency. In all the points mentioned the Targum carries to an extreme a tendency which we meet with in the other ancient versions; it will therefore be unnecessary to revert to the subject again. The process indeed ascends higher up. A rabbinic tradition enumerates eighteen (or eleven) cases where the scribes ' corrected ' the original reading. If Ezra is credited with introducing the corrections, we must bear in mind that in the opinion of the rabbis the ready scribe who headed the Great Synagogue not only collected the sacred writings but also edited their text. As a rule the aim is to wipe out undignified expressions concerning the Deity. To cite one example, the original reading in Habakkuk 1. 12 is said to have been ' Thou diest not ' in the place of the present correction : ' we die not.' There is doubt in the minds of scholars whether some of the instances adduced by the rabbis may not rest on conjecture. On the other hand, there is reason to believe that the text has been altered in a much greater number of places. Thus where the sacred writers spoke of cursing God the text was made to say 'bless' for 'curse.' It is a euphemism pure and simple. Sometimes the alteration betrays itself by its form, as when in Judges 18. 30 a suspended 'n' marks the transformation of Moses, the ancestor of the Levite who ministered at the idolatrous shrine of the Danites, into Manasseh. And when at length the text had become stable, alterations which no longer could be introduced into the text itself were enjoined upon the reader who tacitly substituted a different word in the reading. Thus words which proved offensive to a more refined taste were eliminated. The culminating point, however, was reached in the translations, official or unofficial. The ancients were rather distrustful of the comprehension of the common people, and fidelity to the letter was readily sacrificed when it was felt that the scriptural truth might be obscured and the Word of God be brought into disrepute with the ignorant. If to-day we have largely, though not wholly, outgrown the apprehensions of the ancients, it is because we have a laity trained in a way of looking upon the Scriptures which is itself the outcome of the unremitting efforts of those earlier translators and their authoritative sponsors.

CHAPTER II

THE SEPTUAGINT AND THE LATER GREEK
VERSIONS

Westward had been the march of the Aramaic language, eastward was the progress of the Aramaic Targum. The Babylonian Jewry, with antecedents dating from the time when the mighty Assyrian and Babylonian monarchs transplanted the conquered Israelites and Judeans, was linked to Palestine by the bond of language and culture.

Translations into other Languages spoken by Dispersed Jewry. In the spiritual domain Palestine was the giver and Babylonia the taker; and when at length the leadership had passed on to the Babylonian schools, their scope consisted in adapting and carrying on the learning of Palestine rather than in original production. Farther to the east where the sway of Aramaic terminated, in Elam and in Media, the Scriptures were read in the vernacular of those countries; the translations, however, are no longer extant. There were translations in many more languages, and the rabbis expressly enjoin that the Scriptures may be read in ' all tongues,' that is in all the tongues spoken by Jews in the lands of their dispersion. In the second century before the Christian era a Jewish poet puts in the mouth of the Sibyl the word that all lands and all seas are full of Jews. Whithersoever a Jew migrated, he was welcomed by fellow-Jews; everywhere his God went with him, to every place he carried with him his Scriptures. The rabbis make mention of a version in Coptic, the language of the native population of Egypt inhabiting the rural districts, and it is quite possible that elements of this version are imbedded in the later Church version of the Christian Copts (chapter III). But the greatest and most important of all the translations in the hands of dispersed Jewry was undoubtedly the Greek. The advent of Alexander the Great and the reign of his successors meant outwardly the subjection of the Orient by the Occident, but inwardly the West really succumbed to the East which since time immemorial had exercised a potent influence on the European mind. In the long run a compromise was effected, but in the chaos of diverse nationalities and cultures the Jew stood out distinct. He entered into the sphere of Western culture, and was greatly attracted by it; Greek wisdom, stubbornly resisted in the second pre-Christian century, later on invaded Palestine;

3

but even in the dispersion where the powers of resistance were weakest and the allurements of the Hellenistic culture greatest, the Jew maintained his individuality, and gave back to the world in thousandfold measure what he took from it.   The beauty of Japheth, the father of Javan, dwelt in the tents of Shem.   Through the medium of the Greek the literature of the Jew became the possession of mankind. Without the Greek translation of the Scriptures the Christian conversion of Europe would have been well nigh impossible.   The rabbis recognized the fact, and from their subsequent experience of the havoc wrought to the fortunes of the Jewish people through the Christian schism they may be pardoned for likening the day on which the famous translation saw its light to the day on which the golden calf was fashioned.   A fast-day in Palestine and in the lands swayed by its spiritual dominion, it was a day of rejoicing from year to year in Alexandria where the epoch-making event occurred.   This fact will serve to gauge the diversity of sentiment in Palestine with its eastern dependencies and in the colonies exposed to the immediate influence of Greek culture.

The re-entrance of the Jew into the land of the Pharaohs began at an early period.   Egypt had horses, and Palestine had more people than it could support, and so the Judean kings from Solomon

downward traded their subjects for horseflesh. Jewish soldiers served in the army of Psammetich II
(594-589 B. C.) against the Ethiopians. A large

**Jewish
Settlement
in Egypt.**
body of Jews migrated to Egypt after the
murder of Gedaliah, overruling the oppo-
sition of Jeremiah who was made to ac-
company the exiles. Long before the
conquest of Egypt by Cambyses Jews had been settled as military colonists on the southern frontier of
the realm. Of forceful deportations in the Persian
period and later by the first of the Ptolemies we read
in ancient writers; as late as Roman times Jews
inhabiting a Syrian village know themselves as
Persians in original allegiance. The Jew was in
Egypt before the Greek, but under the second
Ptolemy already the large and influential Jewish community of Alexandria began to exchange their Aramaic speech for the language of the governing race
which was the Greek.

**The Epistle
of Aristeas on
the Origin
of the
Septuagint.**
It is in the reign of the second
Ptolemy, surnamed Philadelphus
(285-247 B. C.), that the translation
of the Law (Pentateuch) into Greek
is placed by the circumstantial nar-
rative known as the Epistle of Aris-
teas which purports to be a contemporary record by
one of the king's courtiers. Nay, according to the

story, the initiative proceeded from the king or rather the king's librarian, Demetrius of Phalerum, who advised that a copy of the Law of the Jews should be deposited in the royal collection of books then already numbering upward of two hundred thousand volumes. An embassy, headed by the captain of the royal bodyguard and Aristeas, is dispatched to Jerusalem with rich presents and a letter to the high priest Eleazar who forwards to the king a copy, richly executed in golden letters, by the hand of seventy-two elders, six from each of the tribes of Israel, men learned in the law and able to translate the Hebrew into Greek. After presentation to the king the company of translators is set to work on an island, far away from the noise of the city. Every day they all translate, each one by himself, a portion of the Law, and then they meet to compare their results and to agree upon a common form. In seventy-two sessions, each lasting until the ninth hour, the work is completed. Demetrius causes the translation to be read to the Jewish community, who receive it warmly and beg that a copy be placed in their hands. A curse is pronounced upon any one who shall make alterations in a work of such excellence and accuracy. The Greek Pentateuch is then read to the king, who expresses delight and surprise, greets the book with a gesture of reverence, and orders that care be taken of it and that it be sacredly guarded.

So far the story, which distinctly asserts that the translators, working singly and with varying results, composed their differences in common sessions, a proceeding natural enough with a company of trans-

Later Embellishments. lators. Subsequently, when the numerous variations in the manuscripts of the translation were observed, it was held that the translators worked in groups of two, and that under the text divergent or alternate renderings were registered. In itself it is a plausible conjecture indeed that, much after the fashion of the King James Version (chapter V), the text was accompanied by a margin in which not only the rejected renderings favored by a minority of the company found a place, but also the more accurate or literal rendition of the original when in accommodation to the genius of the Greek language a freer paraphrase had been adopted in the text. In direct contrast stand the still later embellishments, according to which each translator worked in a cell by himself, and yet their several efforts were found to be identical to the letter—a miracle indeed which has not happened since to any other company of Bible translators! But then the notion prevailed that the seventy-two translators were inspired prophets. Another point in which a later generation disregarded the express language of Aristeas is the inclusion of all the rest of the Scriptures in the translation executed under royal auspices.

Modern scholars are quite agreed that the Epistle of Aristeas cannot be the work of the Gentile courtier, **Modern Doubts.** but is rather the composition of a Jew. The story of the translation of the Law is really incidental to the central theme which is a description of the Jewish people and their land and a glorification of the wisdom of the Jews. Naturally the praise would be more effective when coming from a Gentile whom the writer impersonates. A few errors in detail are pointed out, but in the main it is conceded that the author or the source excerpted by him betrays a remarkable familiarity with the court life of the early Ptolemies. That Philadelphus who was a patron of learning should evince an interest in the Law of the Jews need not be regarded as improbable. Nevertheless the story is rejected as a fabrication, and it is thought more plausible that the initiative belongs to the Jewish community of Alexandria experiencing a need for a version in the Greek. As in the case of Mendelssohn's translation into High German at the close of the eighteenth century (chater VI), the leaders of the community, by means of the Greek translation, set about to prepare the Jew for his entry into the Greek life of the city. If we may at all lay the scheme at the door of the Jewish

CODEX VATICANUS — 4TH CENT.

The most ancient of the manuscripts of the Septuagint

community, another motive will have played into it, namely, to open up the Jewish Law to the inspection of the Gentile population and to convince the world that the Jews possessed a culture which rivalled the wisdom of Hellas. It is quite possible that a copy was presented to the king or that royal sanction was obtained for the translation. It must be added that the Epistle of Aristeas speaks of earlier but inadequate efforts at translation and that, while the Talmud records the legend of the seventy-two translators, it also registers a tradition ascribing the version to five elders.

Internal evidence shows that the five books of the Law could not have been translated by one person. **Style and Dialect.** There is a difference of style and manner of rendering pointing to a number of translators, just how many remains to be ascertained. On the whole the translation must be pronounced a success. It oscillates between a freer method of rendition and a slavish adherence to the letter. The language employed was not the classical Greek, but the Hellenistic dialect which was then rapidly supplanting the older varieties of Greek speech and becoming the uniform literary vehicle among the cultured classes. Naturally the diction of the Scriptures offered difficulties when it had to be cast in a foreign mould; but then the newer Greek had developed many points of style resembling the biblical. At all events it was a happy inspiration to let the inherent beauty of the simple diction of the original shine through the alien garb, and in this respect the manner of those early translators became the model for similar efforts in the future. It may be that a Greek with more classic tastes might find the thinly disguised Hebraisms barbaric; at the same time there attached to the translation the merit of bringing the peculiar literature of the Jew to the comprehension of the plain people. In Alexandria as well as in Palestine the Bible, whether in Greek or Aramaic, was to be the people's book.

The Translators' Knowledge of Hebrew.   In the main the translators understood their Hebrew well, and admirably hit the sense of the original. Tradition was on the whole still a living thing. The meaning of words was derived from the dictionary of life; the translators made, or rather were, their own dictionary. The vicissitudes through which the Jewish people had passed, the change of speech being not the least of them, will explain how it happened that at a given point tradition had been cut in twain and much was suffered to be effaced from the memory of the Jews. In all such cases the translators sought to approximate the true meaning. Take for instance the rarer words denoting precious stones or certain animals and plants which were identified with a varying degree of certainty or probability. There is nothing improbable in the notion that the translators came from Palestine. Like the translator of Sirach in a subsequent period, they acquired or perfected their knowledge of Greek on settling in Egypt; and like the same disciple of the wise, they occasionally committed those blunders that mar a piece of work otherwise meritorious. Certainly from the schools in Palestine came those bits of interpretation evolved by generations of expounders that cannot be said to be obvious in themselves. And as the Palestinian interpretation was largely expressed through the oral Targum, the many coincidences between the latter and the Greek version become intelligible. At times the translators may have indulged in concessions to the spirit of the time and environment. The talmudic tradition enumerates thirteen deliberate alterations introduced by the translators; only a few, however, may be verified from the extant manuscripts of the version. The most interesting case is the circumlocution 'rough-foot' for 'hare' in Leviticus 11. 6, because the ordinary Greek appellation of the hare (*lagos*), it was feared, might be offensive to the royal family, the first Ptolemy being surnamed Lagi. As the rabbis expressed themselves, the king's wife (or mother) bore the name of hare. Traces of the influence of Greek philosophy have been detected, but they are insignificant.

The translation of the seventy-two reputed elders has come to be named for short that of the Seventy **Translations** or Septuagint (from the Latin *septua-* **of the other** *ginta* = seventy). The name clung **Parts of the** not only to the version of the Penta- **Scriptures.** teuch, but also to that of the whole of the Scriptures. For in due sequel the other parts of the Scriptures likewise were translated into Greek, naturally at different times and by different hands. In the whole, certain groups of books stand out clearly as the work of single translators. It goes without saying that the manner of translation differs, ranging from the freest paraphrase, as in Proverbs and Job, to the most slavishly literal translation, as in Samuel and Kings. The translator of Job excels as a Greek writer, showing an acquaintance with the master-products of Greek poetry. He considered himself at liberty to shorten the original considerably, omitting some eight hundred lines. Isaiah is the worst translated book. Just when the whole of the Scriptures was completed in Greek is a matter of uncertainty. Roughly speaking the process of translating the Bible into Greek covered a period of a century or a century and a half. When the grandson of Jesus son of Sirach arrived in Egypt in the year 132 B. C., he found ' the Law and the Prophets and the remainder of the books ' in Greek. The Law and the Prophets are definite terms covering the first two parts of the Hebrew Scriptures, the second division containing not only the prophetical writings (Isaiah, Jeremiah, Ezekiel, the Twelve), but also the historical books (Joshua–Kings) which incorporate records of prophetic activity and, moreover, were believed to have been compiled by inspired prophets.   As for ' the remainder of the books,' the appellation is no more vague than the name Ketubim, ' Writings,' by which the third division goes.   Incidentally the Siracid reveals that the purpose of translation was to enable those that resided in a foreign land to obtain instruction and wisdom from books otherwise beyond their comprehension.

Inclusion of Books wanting in the Hebrew Canon. And so the Wisdom of the son of Sirach, which in Palestine and Babylonia hovered on the borderland between writings avowedly sacred and those which remained outside the biblical collection, found a place in the Greek Bible, and with it many more books, some of which were from the outset composed in Greek and were therefore unknown in Palestine, while others, though originally written in Hebrew or Aramaic, had not been accorded scriptural rank at home. All these writings comprise, so to speak, the fourth and fifth part of the Scriptures, known as Apocrypha or books withdrawn from public use and at best tolerated only for private reading, and Pseudepigrapha, *i. e.,* spurious writings assigned to authors of the past and for the most part sectarian products deviating from the path of conduct and doctrine marked out by the authoritative leaders in Palestine. If we to-day are in a position to read in the First Book of the Maccabees, for instance, the exploits of Judas Maccabeus, ' who made Jacob glad with his acts, and his memorial is blessed for ever,' we owe a debt of gratitude to the Christian Church which, having received the Greek Scriptures at the hands of the Greek-speaking Jews of the empire, with pious zeal kept them intact, and rescued from oblivion literary records of near-scriptural rank.

The Later Greek Versions. The passing on of the Greek Bible to the Christian Church was itself the cause of the rise of a series of newer Greek versions or revisions dating for the most part from the second Christian century. The Jews looked askance at the older translation which was marred by evident blunders and moreover differed at times widely from the recognized text of the original. Here and there, too, there had crept into the copies Christian interpolations, as when in Psalm

96. 10 the words 'from the cross' were added to the sentence 'the Lord reigneth.' Yet Greek was the language of the Jew of Asia Minor, Northern Africa, and Europe. The first place among the later Greek versions unquestionably belongs to the effort **Aquila.** of Aquila, a proselyte from Pontus, who worked under the eye of the celebrated Palestinian teachers, Rabbi Eliezer and Rabbi Joshua. Though his mastery of the Greek language was such as only a native Greek could command, he chose with painstaking fidelity to produce a word-for-word translation in which not only the sequence of words in the original was faithfully reproduced, but even Hebrew word formations were imitated, and every particle received an equivalent. The effect of the whole was naturally barbaric, and it was said of him that he translated 'not words, but syllables.' The Palestinian authorities, however, lauded the translator in superlative terms; the accuracy with which the original was followed outweighed all considerations of style. The consecration of the letter was the Synagogue's weapon of defence against the nascent Church; while the copies of the Septuagint made by Christian hands became more and more disfigured by scribal corruptions, the text of the original was zealously guarded by the Synagogue, and the scribes lovingly counted every letter that no alteration should

creep in. Moreover, the Septuagint, whether from
the start or in consequence of Christian manipula-
tions, contained renderings which were offensive to
the Jew, as when in Isaiah 7. 14 the mother of
Immanuel was spoken of as a 'virgin.' Aquila
naturally substituted, in accord with the Hebrew, ' a
young woman '; he equally avoided as a rendering
for ' Messiah ' the Greek *Christos,* which had become
a name imparting to the Church its very appellation, selecting in its stead an inoffensive synonym.
Aquila's translation continued in use among Greek-
speaking Jews to a late date, and the emperor Jus-
tinian (527-565) granted permission for its employment in the synagogues.

Symmachus.   To offset Aquila's literalism, Symmachus, a Jewish Christian of the
Ebionite sect, produced a translation which was in
the nature of a paraphrase aiming rather at the sense
than at a verbal rendering. Nevertheless he made
frequent use of Aquila, exactly as was done by
Theodotion.   another contemporary, Theodotion, like
Aquila himself a convert to Judaism,
who, however, struck a happy medium, combining
elegance of diction with fidelity to the original. These
three translations or rather revisions of the Septuagint—there were several others whose authors remained unknown—were made use of by the two

great fathers of the Church, Origen (185-254) and Jerome (346-420), in their work of improving the current Church Bible. Though both are reported as having studied Hebrew, Origen turning for advice to Rabbi Hillel brother of Rabbi Judah II the Patriarch and Jerome having for his teacher a scholar by the name of Barannina, they relied for their information about the contents of the Hebrew original, or, as they expressed themselves, the ' Hebrew

Origen's Edition of the Greek Scriptures.
truth,' mainly upon the Three, Aquila serving as a dictionary, as it were, Symmachus as a commentary, and Theodotion as a translation. Origen transcribed them (as well as the other anonymous versions) in his monumental edition of the Greek Bible, where Aquila occupied the third column next to the Hebrew in the original square characters and in Greek transliteration, thus enabling the student to pronounce every Hebrew word and at once to ascertain its meaning; then came the free Symmachus, then the text of the Septuagint, then Theodotion, then in the remaining columns the other versions wherever they were available. The Septuagint text occupying the fifth column was entirely recast so as to square with the ' Hebrew truth ': gaps were filled up from the Three, in particular from Theodotion; additions not found in the Hebrew,

though copied, were marked as unwarranted; proper names made unrecognizable in the current manuscripts were adjusted to the Hebrew text in the later pronunciation; other corrections were boldly introduced; the sequence of the Hebrew was restored, not only where the Hebrew text had been disturbed on a large scale, as in Exodus and Jeremiah, but almost in every line. The bulky work, known chiefly as Hexapla (a book of six columns), was deposited in the library of Caesarea, the nucleus of which had been formed by Origen out of the biblical collection possessed by Symmachus and acquired by a certain Juliana; there it was inspected by Jerome, but after

Remains of the Hexapla. a century or so all traces of it were lost. A few leaves of a copy containing the Psalms were recently discovered in Milan; other fragments were found in the Cairo Genizah, the contents of which it was the merit of the late Dr. Schechter to discover and transfer to the University of Cambridge; from the same Genizah came the long lost Hebrew original of Ecclesiasticus, as also a fragment of the translation of Aquila. With the exception of Theodotion's Daniel which was read in Christian churches in preference to the older but freer Greek version, and which is therefore extant as a whole, all our other knowledge of the later Greek versions comes from stray notes on the margin of

PALIMPSEST OF THE CAIRO GENIZAH

The upper writing in Hebrew of the 11th cent., the lower in Greek of the
6th cent. Contains Aquila's version

Septuagint manuscripts, excerpts made by learned owners from Origen's great work, and is naturally fragmentary. It is after all mainly to the Christian Church that we owe whatever knowledge of them we may possess; for, while, as the Cairo leaves prove, in the earlier Christian centuries copies of the Greek translations later than the Septuagint were current in Egypt, subsequently, when the Greek had ceased to be spoken by Egyptian Jewry, the parchment was turned by copyists to a use nearer home after the ink had been washed away.

But before we dismiss the subject of Greek translations of the Scriptures, mention must be made of **Medieval Jewish Translations in Greek.** a learned effort by a Jew of the fourteenth century to render the Bible into classical (Attic) Greek (the Aramaic passages of Daniel he gave in the Doric dialect); naturally he embodied the results of Jewish exegetical labors then accessible (chapter IV). On the other hand, the translation in modern Greek and in Hebrew characters which accompanies the Hebrew text of the Pentateuch printed in Constantinople 1547 (see below, chapter IV) was to serve a practical purpose, 'that it might be useful to young Jews and that they might accustom themselves to speak correctly.'

CHAPTER III

ANCIENT CHRISTIAN TRANSLATIONS

For nearly two centuries the Christian Church knew no other Scriptures than the collection taken over from the Jews. Only towards the end of the second century was the New Testament placed on an equal footing with the Old, and both together made up the Bible of the Catholic Church. The **Christian Translations.** two oldest Christian translations of the Hebrew Scriptures, dating from, or at least in their beginnings ascending to, the second century, are the Syriac and the Latin. The Syriac language is really a variety of the Aramaic; it was spoken in the north of Syria and Upper Mesopotamia, and it survives to this day in certain circumscribed localities in a multitude of modern forms, chief among which is the Urmi dialect, first reduced to writing in the year 1836 by Dr. Perkins, an American Presbyterian missionary, who translated the Bible afresh into it. There are several translations in the older Syriac, but the oldest and noblest, frequently called 'the Queen of Versions,' is known as Peshitta, which means ' the Simple,' that is the common and widely current. It was made from the Hebrew with the assistance of Jews, combining with fidelity to the original elegance of style and **The Peshitta.** embodying, notably in the Pentateuch, elements of interpretation rooted in Jewish tradition. The translation of Chronicles reads like a Targum, just as conversely the Targum to Proverbs was borrowed by the Jews from the Peshitta (chapter I). Intercourse between Jews and Christians was facilitated in those regions by the employment of the same vernacular. Nevertheless the version as we have it to-day is largely intermixed with alterations made on the basis of the Septuagint which was the Church Bible. The Psalter in particular is permeated with Greek influence, as is natural with a book used in the liturgy.

Obscure though the beginnings of the Latin Church translation may be, it is clear that the need for it arose in the provinces, specifically in North **The** Africa, rather than in Rome where Greek **Old Latin.** was the language of the Church in its early days. It is really not permissible to speak of one translation; parallel versions cropped up in various localities. We have the testimony of Augustine (354-430) that as different copies of the Greek were chanced upon, diverse translations were

made with varying degrees of skill. What is common
to all of them is the character of the Latin which is not
the classical, but of the rustic variety such as was
used in the popular speech throughout the confines
of the empire, leading over to the later forms known
as the Romanic languages. The new religion—
Christianity—had been embraced by the humble and
poor, the scriptural message was for the people, the
broad masses, and it was fitting that the Bible everywhere should speak their language. As the Church
in the capital became Latinized, the divergences in
the copies of the Latin version and the crudity of its
Jerome's   diction called for a revision. At the bid-
Revisions.   ding of the Roman bishop Damasus the
task was undertaken by Jerome (346-
420). While in Rome (in the year 383) Jerome
slightly retouched the Psalter, which revision Damasus at once introduced in the liturgy; it is still in
use at St. Peter's. A second and more thorough
revision on the basis of Origen's text in the Hexapla
(chapter II) was executed nine years later at Bethle-
hem; this edition, known as the Gallican Psalter,
gained first admission in Gaul; it is also the rendition
incorporated in the ordinary editions of the Vulgate.
In Palestine, however, Jerome set about to acquire a
knowledge of the Hebrew by the aid of Jewish
teachers, and under their guidance, as well as with the

help of the later Greek versions (chapter II), he produced a new translation which under the name Vulgate was destined to become the acknowledged Bible of the Catholic Church and of Western Europe. Altogether fifteen years were spent on that work, the various books coming out at intervals in response to

The Vulgate. the promptings of friends. The Solomonic writings were done in three days, Tobit in one day, Judith over night, the two latter from an Aramaic copy which his Jewish teacher read off in Hebrew translation, while a scribe took down the Latin at Jerome's dictation. The Psalter he rendered now, for the third time, from the Hebrew; this newer version, however, remained outside the Vulgate. Certain of the apocryphal books (chapter II) were left by Jerome in their old unrevised form. Like all innovations, Jerome's new translation gained ground but slowly; but as time went on it superseded the older Latin versions, until at length in the fourth session of the Council of Trent (April 8, 1546) it was pronounced the only authentic Latin translation to be used in public lessons, disputations, sermons, and expositions. Unfortunately the text was vitiated through admixture of readings from the Old Latin, and to this day the Catholic Church has been solicitous in purifying the version. In the main the Vulgate is characterized by a Latin diction which aims at being classical. The co-ordination of clauses peculiar to Hebrew construction is turned into stately periods, frequently the original is contracted, and at times words are added for the sake of clarity. To bring out the sense, and if needs be by paraphrase, was Jerome's chief concern. In the Douai Bible (1609), which is the authorized Catholic rendition of the Vulgate into English, the character of Jerome's style is still largely preserved, a factor which together with the many Latinisms employed by the translators, Catholic exiles from England, differentiates it, to its disadvantage, from the Anglican version of 1611. Modern Catholic Churchmen candidly admit the superior diction of the latter, and

Church Translations in other Languages. in their revisions freely borrow from it. Of course, the Catholic English Bible remains a tertiary product such as the Old Latin was denominated by Jerome. Nevertheless, in the official service of the Church the greater part of the Scriptures is read in a translation directly resting on the original, while the Coptic (in various dialects), Gothic, Armenian, Ethiopic, Georgian, as well as the English translations prior to the Reformation, are tertiary products, based on the Greek or the Latin of Jerome; the Arabic versions were made from the Greek, Syriac, and Coptic, and one Persian translation goes back to the

Peshitta. However, in the Coptic and Ethiopic there are elements taken directly from the Hebrew (chapter II). The date of all these Church versions varies, ranging from the third to the thirteenth century. The Gothic version was contemporary with Jerome; there is a letter extant from the pen of the most erudite among the fathers of the Church to two Gothic scholars who, unfamiliar with the languages of the original, experienced difficulty in accounting for the differences between Jerome's newer version and the Greek. The Church father welcomes with delight this interest in the Scriptures from the far-off north, coming at a time 'when polished Greece is asleep.' With the Psalmist he calls out: 'Their sound is gone forth into all the earth, and their words to the end of the world' (Psalm 19.5 according to the Septuagint).

CHAPTER IV

JEWISH TRANSLATIONS IN THE MIDDLE AGES

The rabbis speak of two kinds of Hebrew, the language of the Scriptures and the language of the wise in which the Mishnah and the cognate literature are composed. The latter has been wrongly likened to the scholars' Latin of the Middle Ages; it is rather a natural outgrowth from the older language. In-**The Precursors of the Science of Scriptural Interpretation.** deed the later writings of the Hebrew Bible and the earliest legal norms known as halakahs are indited in a transitional style half-biblical half-mishnic. Many words which the biblical writers had no occasion to use have been preserved in the later literature. The Jewish Book of Prayer has noble pieces of pure Hebrew. Thus for the most part a living tradition of the Hebrew language continued long after it had vanished from the mouth of the people. The rabbis themselves knew their Bible well. There is not a page of the Talmud, a chapter of the Midrash, that is not replete with biblical quotations. The genealogical chapters of Chronicles with their mere lists of names were as

נמוגפלשתכלךממעֿוֿ
עשןבאואין־בודדֿ ל
במועדיוֿ ומהֿ ־־־ יענה
מלאביגויכי יחוה יסד
ציוןובחיחסועני עמו
משאמואב
כיבליל שֿדֿ ד־ער מואב
נדמהכובלילשֿדֿ ר קיר
מואבנדמהֿ עלהֿ הבית
ורבֿ נוהבֿ מותֿ לבכיֿ עֿל־
נבוֿ ועֿ למידֿ בֿ א־מואב
יילילבכלראשיוקרֿ חֿ ה
וכלזקןגֿ דוֿ עהֿ בֿ חוצֿ ותֿ
חגרושקֿ עֿ ל־־־גֿ גותיהֿ
וברֿ חבתהֿ כלהֿ וֿ זֿ יֿ ליל
יֿרֿ דבֿ בֿ כֿ יֿ וֿ תֿ שֿ עֿ קֿ חֿ שבֿ ון
ואלעֿ לֿ הֿ עדֿ יֿ הֿ ץֿ נשמע
קולם עלֿ כֿ ןֿ חלֿ צֿ מואב
יריעונפשורעהֿ לֿ וֿ
לבי למואביזֿ עֿ קֿ בֿ רֿ יֿ חֿ ה
עדצער עגלֿ תֿ שֿ לֿ שֿ יֿ הֿ

כי מעלֿהֿ הלוחיתבֿ בֿ כי
יעלהבוֿ כֿ יֿ כֿ יֿ דֿ רֿ ךֿ חורֿ נֿ ֿם
זֿ עֿ קֿ תֿ שֿ בֿ ר יעֿ עֿ רויכֿ עֿ רֿ יֿ
נמריֿ ם משמוֿ תֿ יֿ וֿ חֿ וֿ ־כֿ יֿ
יבֿ שֿ חֿ צֿ ורכֿ לֿ הֿ דֿ שֿ א֑
ירקלאאחֿ יֿ הֿ עֿ לֿ כֿ ן֨ ֿיֿתֿ רֿ הֿ
עֿ שֿ הֿ ופֿ קֿ דֿ תֿ םֿ ֿעֿ לֿ נֿ חֿ ל
הֿ עֿ רֿ בֿ יֿ ם ישֿ אֿ וֿ םֿ ־כֿ יֿ ־הֿ
הֿ קֿ יֿ פֿ הֿ חֿ זֿ עֿ קֿ הֿ ־אֿ תֿ ־
גֿ בֿ ולֿ מואב יעֿ דֿ ־אֿ גֿ לֿ יֿ ֿם
יֿ לֿ לֿ תֿ הֿ ובֿ אֿ ר־ אילים֒
יֿ לֿ לֿ תֿ הֿ ־כי מֿ יֿ דֿ יֿ מֿ וֿ ןֿ מֿ לֿ אֿ ֽו־
דֿ ם כֿ יֿ אֿ שֿ יֿ ֿת עֿ ל־דֿ יֿ מֿ וֿ ןֿ
נוֿ סֿ פֿ וֿ תֿ ־לֿ פֿ לֿ יֿ טֿ תֿ מוֿ אֿ ֿב
אֿ רֿ יֿ הֿ ־ולֿ שֿ אֿ רֿ יֿ תֿ אֿ דֿ מֿ הֿ ־
שֿ לֿ חֿ וֿ ־כֿ ר־מֿ שֿ ֿל־־־אֿ רֿ ץֿ ֿ
מֿ סֿ לֿ עֿ ־מֿ דֿ בֿ רֿ הֿ ֿ־אֿ ל־הֿ רֿ ־
בֿ תֿ ־צֿ יֿ וֿ ֿן ֿוֿ הֿ יֿ הֿ כֿ ־עֿ וֿ ףֿ ־נֿ וֿ דֿ ֿד
קֿ ֿן מֿ שֿ לֿ ח־תֿ הֿ יֿ נֿ הֿ ־בֿ נֿ וֿ תֿ ֿ
מוֿ אֿ ֿב מֿ עֿ בֿ רֿ ותֿ ־לֿ אֿ רֿ נֿ וֿ ֿן־
הֿ בֿ יֿ אֿ וֿ ־עֿ צֿ הֿ ־עֿ שֿ וֿ ־פֿ לֿ יֿ לֿ הֿ ֿ

CODEX PETROPOLITANUS — 916 C. E.

With superlinear vocalization and Masoretic notes

familiar to them as a chapter from Deuteronomy or a
psalm. They were not strangers to simpler grammatical observations, and the finer points of the scriptural idiom did not escape their attention. Nevertheless their interest in the Bible was mainly practical:
Talmud. it served as a basis for legal deductions or
moral lessons. The sea of the Talmud
threatened to submerge the fountain-head out of
which it had sprung. The talmudic teachers readily
conceded their ignorance in matters of spelling and
the like, and left the care of the sacred text to the
elementary schoolmasters. To these humbler scholars we owe the invention of the vowel and accent
points in which was deposited a goodly portion of
the traditional pronunciation and interpretation of
the biblical Word; it is they who built up in suc-
Masorah. cessive stages the Masorah, that gigantic
system of lists now on the margin of
copies of the sacred text prepared for private use,
now in independent works, a veritable fence ward-
ing off the innovations not sanctioned by tradition.
In the school of Tiberias these studies were particularly cultivated. The two great Masoretes, Ben
Asher and Ben Naphtali, emerging towards the close
of the gaonic period, are already semi-grammarians.
The Karaitic schism with its revolt against the Talmud paved the way for a return to the Scriptures in

which the Rabbanites were not slow to take a leading part.   Naturally the first attempts signified a

**The Return
to the
Scriptures.**

groping in the darkness.   Kalir, the
great liturgist of the eighth century,
strives after biblical diction, but his
perverted notions of the laws of gram-
mar render his poetic productions, rich in thought as
they are, exceedingly unedifying on the side of language.   The schoolmasters had done well in their
way; now it was the task of the scholar to resurrect
petrified tradition by the application of the scientific

**The Scientific
Method of
Interpretation.**

method.   The men to whom it fell to
construct the Hebrew grammar and
the Hebrew dictionary and the Bible
commentary and Bible criticism were
at home in the post-biblical literature, that great
store-house of linguistic material; they knew the two
foremost sister-languages of the Hebrew, the Aramaic from their study of Targum and Talmud, and
the Arabic which they spoke; they were versed in the
great Arabic literature; they were familiar with the
Koran and the poets; they studied the native Arab
grammarians and lexicographers, who with great in-
dustry and finesse of perception had built up an accurate science of their rich language—apt pupils of the
Syrian grammarians whose efforts rested upon the
lore of Greece where grammar as a science had its
origin.

The first among these Bible students was he whom posterity celebrated as the first spokesman in all the branches of Jewish learning, the Gaon Saadya, that formidable foe of Karaism (892-942). Master of the law (halakah), liturgical poet, theological controversialist, philosopher, he, like many another **Saadya.** spiritual leader in Jewry in a similar crisis, realized that the study of the Scriptures must be the corner-stone of Jewish learning. To aid in a correct handling of the Hebrew language by the poets of the synagogue, he wrote a Hebrew grammar and a dictionary of the sacred language. As a direct help to the understanding of the Scriptures, he collected ninety words which occur but once or rarely in the Bible, ' having neither brother nor friend,' and showed how, by the aid of the later Hebrew or the cognate Arabic, their meaning became clear. To cite but one example: Isaiah 14. 12, at the end, he recovers for the Hebrew verb the mean- **His** ing ' cast lots upon ' in the place of ' lay low ' **Arabic** still found in the current translations and dictionaries; the corresponding noun, mean- **Version.** ing ' lot,' he located in the Mishnah. By far transcending in importance was his translation of the Scriptures into Arabic, in some books accompanied by a commentary. Though not a paraphrase, the version is by no means literal. Where necessary a word is added to bring out the sense clearly; several verses are frequently joined together in a syntactical nexus, and thus, though the original coloring is lost, the translation gains in lucidity. With a view to the same end a positive Arabic equivalent is introduced where the meaning of the Hebrew is doubtful, in order not to awaken in the laity the thought that there are obscure expressions in the Scriptures. What is principally aimed at is clarity and elegant diction. Ancient names of places are modernized. Though an upholder of tradition, Saadya emancipates himself from the forced interpretation of the rabbis, thus breaking ground for a rational exposition based on grammar and an adequate observation of the usage of words within the compass of the entire Scriptures. He does not consider himself bound by the marginal corrections (variants) of the Masoretes (chapter VIII), and frequently embodies in his translation the textual reading (ketib) in the text. Though naturally not free from faults, Saadya's version served as a mine in the hands of successive generations of Bible students; but it was intended in the first instance for the people, the Jews in the vast domain of Arabic culture; to this day it is read by the Yemenite Jews, who, driven from their home by persecution and employed as common laborers in the Jewish colonies of Palestine, bring with them the

Scriptures in the Hebrew original, the Targum neatly pointed, and Saadya's Arabic translation.

The Babylonian center of Jewry was now in the last stages of dissolution; another was preparing in the West in the Iberian peninsula, the North African coast serving as a bridge. On the banks of the Ebro, in Tortosa, under the patronage of the Jewish statesman Hasdai Ibn Shaprut, Menahem ben Saruk (about 960) worked out in Hebrew the first complete dictionary of the Scriptures. Unfortunately he had not hit upon the right understanding of the structure of Hebrew; he was attacked by Dunash, a pupil of Saadya's, who won over the rich and powerful Maecenas. The fame of both soon spread beyond the confines of the Moorish dominions. In Northern France a new school of Jewish learning, branching off from the seat of talmudic erudition established in the Rhenish provinces by Gershom 'the Light of Exile,' was in course of construction. Solomon son of Isaac, better known as Rashi (died 1105), the great commentator of the Talmud, found leisure to write a commentary on the Bible. His exposition of the Pentateuch in particular became in time the most popular and widely used, and ever after it meant the sum of lay education for a Jew to have read his Homesh (Penta-

The First Complete Hebrew Dictionary.

Dunash.

Rashi: the Popular Commentator.

teuch) with Rashi. What made for the popularity of
this commentary was its intermediate attitude between the traditional interpretation of the rabbis and
the more modern rational exegesis. In grammatical
matters, Menahem and his critic are Rashi's chief
guides. The feud which ensued between the disciples
of both had not yet become known outside Spain; the
French commentators worked in isolation, producing
some good results, and the aged Rashi confessed to
his grandson, Samuel son of Meir, that, were he at leisure, he should have to revise his own commentary in
accordance with the newer interpretations coming up
daily. Interspersed in Rashi's commentary, as in all
the productions of the French school, are renditions
of difficult Hebrew words and phrases in French; we
also possess independent glossaries, thus amounting
to a partial Jewish version of the Scriptures in
French which constitutes one of the early records
of the language. Catholic priests who sought out
Rashi brought him a knowledge of Jerome's Latin
version; conversely, Rashi's commentary was excerpted in Latin by the apostate Nicholas de Lyra
(died 1340) whose ' Postillae Perpetuae,' printed in
1471-2, exercised a potent influence on Luther's
German translation of the Bible (chapter V).

Meanwhile a revolution had been wrought in
Spain. To a disciple of Menahem, Judah son of

David Hayyuj, who taught in Cordova at the beginning of the eleventh century, fell the momentous and

**Hayyuj:
the ' First
Grammarian.'**
epoch-making discovery of the funda-
mental character of Hebrew root structure. The memory of the ' first grammarian,' as Hayyuj was called, was
cherished by posterity; his system was improved in
detail by Jonah Ibn Janah, ' the greatest of medieval

**Ibn Janah:
the ' Greatest
of Medieval
Hebraists.'**
Hebraists,' in the first half of the
eleventh century. A physician by profession, he employed his leisure in deep-
ening the newly won scientific study of
the Bible through a series of contro-
versial treatises, but chiefly through his double work
containing a grammar and dictionary of the Bible languages. Both Hayyuj and Ibn Janah composed their
works in Arabic; their influence was therefore confined for the time being to their immediate circle,
though later on their efforts were made accessible to a
wider public through translation into Hebrew. How
seriously these pioneers in Bible interpretation took
their task may be gauged by what Ibn Janah tells of
of his teacher Isaac son of Saul : he was in the habit of
reciting the one hundred and forty-third psalm in his
nightly devotions, but he ceased to do so when he
found that he was unable to interpret a certain word
in the ninth verse. Gifted with keen observation and

a fine insight into the spirit of the Hebrew, Ibn Janah
became the guide of posterity; his works were freely
excerpted, but in the course of time were forgotten,
until they were resuscitated in the nineteenth century.
W. Robertson Smith laments the fact that this fine
scholar has been neglected by expositors subsequent
to Gesenius (chapter VI). The work so auspiciously
begun by Ibn Janah was carried on by men of genius;
the Scriptures were now better understood, and the
Hebrew of the Bible became a vehicle of poetic productions, metrical and rhymed after the manner of
the Arabs, under the hands of famed singers, such as
Solomon Ibn Gabirol and Judah ha-Levi. The learning of the farthest West, for which Saadya in the

Hai Gaon. East had laid the foundations and to
which another Eastern Gaon, Hai (died
1038), before the flickering flame of the Babylonian
schools became wholly extinct, had made a notable
contribution, was at once carried to fruition and dis-

Ibn Ezra: seminated through the darkest abodes
the Scientific of Jewry by Abraham son of Meir Ibn
Commentator. Ezra (1092-1167). A born wanderer,
this profound scholar, poet, and philosopher traveled far and wide, away from his native
city Toledo in Spain through North Africa and the
Orient, to Rome, to France, to England, ' sojourning
everywhere, composing works and laying bare the

secrets of knowledge.' In 1140 we find him at Rome
writing a Hebrew grammar and commentaries on the
Five Scrolls and Job; at Lucca in 1145 he defends
the Gaon Saadya, comments on Isaiah, and begins
his exposition of the Pentateuch; at Mantua in the
same year he produces another grammatical work;
at Beziers in 1155 he writes on the divine name; the
next years find him at Dreux, in France, busy with
commentaries on Daniel, the Twelve, Exodus, and
the remainder of the Pentateuch. In his preface to
the Torah he defines his exposition as ' bound up with
grammar.' Ibn Ezra was a thorough-going rational-
ist; his guarded remarks on the Babylonian author-
ship of the Second Isaiah (an opinion advanced, as he
tells us, by a predecessor) and on the anachronisms in
the Pentateuch pointing to a post-Mosaic compilation
of the Torah make him a forerunner of criticism and
the inspirer of the theories propounded by Spinoza.
His commentaries are for the most part written in a
succinct and at times enigmatic style, but they are
replete with references to older expositors, and are
stimulating throughout, scintillating with keen wit,
and everywhere testifying to a fine perception of the
scriptural language and subject-matter. Next to
Rashi's Bible commentary, that by Ibn Ezra enjoyed
great popularity, though his influence extended pri-
marily to the scholars. Like Rashi, Ibn Ezra wrote

5

in Hebrew. On his wanderings he made many friends; in France he met Rashi's other grandson,

Rabbenu Tam. Jacob son of Meir, surnamed Tam, who still operated with Menahem and Dunash, defending the former against the latter, but independently arriving pretty nearly at the conclusions long anticipated by the 'first grammarian.' Nowhere was Ibn Ezra's appearance more welcomed than in the Provence, the bridge between the southern peninsula and the north. A hundred and fifty years later a Provençal scholar of Beziers reports thus concerning the profound impression made by Ibn Ezra's advent there: 'Our fathers told us of the joy with which the great of our land, its pious men and rabbis, received Ibn Ezra when his wanderings brought him to them. He opened the eyes of the inhabitants of these regions, and wrote for them commentaries and other works.' In the Provence Ibn

The Kimhis. Ezra's seed yielded rich fruit; Joseph Kimhi (about 1150), whose native home was Spain, and his two sons, Moses and David, who lived by tutoring, brought to consummation the labor of three centuries, and though much work was done after them, it remained for the most part of an inferior character. David (1160-1235) in particular, the author of a masterly Hebrew grammar and dictionary, became the famed teacher of posterity far beyond the confines of his own people. When at the revival of learning in the early sixteenth century Christian Churchmen, following in the footsteps of Jerome in the fourth century, sought instruction in

David Kimhi. Hebrew at the hands of Jewish scholars, all that these teachers could impart to them was a digest of the labors of David Kimhi. In 1506 the humanist Reuchlin wrote the first Hebrew grammar and dictionary produced by a Christian scholar, and his teachers were Jacob Jehiel Loans and Obadiah Sforno. Sebastian Münster and Paul Fagius were the pupils of Elias Levita (1469-1548), a versatile man who became the link between Kimhi and the Christian Hebraists.

The influence of Kimhi, as we shall have occasion to see later (chapter V), may be traced in every line

Versions in Persian. of the Anglican translation of 1611. His fame spread early; in the far-away East he was studied, his interpretation being made the basis of a Persian translation done by a Jew about 1400, of which the books of Isaiah, Jeremiah, and (in part) Ezekiel are extant (in a Paris manuscript; published by Lagarde in 1884). Of a later date is the Persian version of the Pentateuch by Rabbi Jacob Tawos, printed at Constantinople in 1546 and reproduced in the fourth volume of Walton's Polyglot. Of two Greek versions by Jewish

authors mention was made above (chapter II) ; the
one was certainly influenced by Kimhi, while the
other served the purposes of Jews in the Byzantine empire.   The edition in which the latter was
printed (Constantinople 1547) contains the Pentateuch together with the Haftarot (Prophetical lessons) and the Five Scrolls (Song of Songs, Ruth,
Lamentations, Ecclesiastes, Esther) in the Hebrew,
in the Targum ' which every child of Israel is enjoined to read,' in Neo-Greek and in Spanish (both
in Hebrew characters), ' the two languages in vogue
among our people in the captivity, the remnant of
Judah and Israel dwelling in Turkish lands,' accompanied by Rashi's commentary.   The

In Spanish.   Spanish translation rests upon previous
labors executed in Spain in the preceding centuries.
In 1422 Rabbi Moses Arragel translated the Bible
from the Hebrew original at the bidding of a prince
of the Church and with the assistance of Francis-
can clerics.   The famous Ferrara Bible in Spanish
(printed in 1553) was a revision of that version; it
was edited by Abraham Usque (otherwise Duarte
Pinel) and published at the expense of Yom Tob
Atias (otherwise Jeronimo de Vargas).   It is interesting that in certain copies, as a concession to
Christian readers, the rendering ' virgin ' is found
in Isaiah 7. 14, while those which were intended for

במדבר

ומליל יי עם משה במדברא דסיני במשכן זמנא בחד לירחא תנינא בשתא תניתא למפקהון מארעא דמצרים למימר: קבילו ית חושבן כל כנשתא דבני ישראל לזרעיתהון לבית אבהתהון במנין שמהן כל דכורא לגולגלתהון: מבר עשרין שנין ולעילא כל נפיק חילא בישראל תמנון יתהון לחיליהון את ואהרן: ועמכון יהון גברא גברא לשבטא גבר ריש לבית אבהתוהי הוא: ואלין שמהת גובריא די יקומון עמכון לראובן אליצור בר שדיאור: לשמעון שלומיאל בר צורישדי: ליהודה נחשון בר עמינדב: ליששכר נתנאל בר צוער: לזבולן אליאב בר חילן: לבני יוסף לאפרים אלישמע בר עמיהוד למנשה גמליאל בר פדהצור: לבנימן אבידן בר גדעוני: לדן אחיעזר בר עמישדי:

פ פ פ

אי הבלו יי א משה אין דיזיירטו
די סיני אין טיינדה דיל פלאזו
אין אונו אל מיש איל שיגונדו
אין איל אניו איל שיגונדו אשו
שאליר די טיירה די מצרים פור
דיזיר: ריסיביד לה קואינטה
די טודה קונפנייא די חיגוש די
ישראל אשוש ליבאנייש א קשת
דישוש פדריש פור קואינטה די
נומבריש טודו מאנו אשו קביסש
: די איידאד די וינטי אנייוש אי
אריבה טודו שאליין פונשארו א
אין ישראל קונטרידיש אאילייוש
אשוש פונשארדוש טו אי אהרן:
אי קונבוש שיראן וארון וארון

פ

וידבר יהוה אל־משה
במדבר סיני באהל
מועד באחד לחדש
השני בשנה השנית
לצאתם מארץ מצרים לאמר:
שאו את־ראש כל־עדת בני־
ישראל למשפחתם לבית א
אבתם במספר שמות כל־זכר
לגלגלתם: מבן עשרים שנה
ומעלה כל־יצא צבא בישראל
תפקדו אתם לצבאתם אתה
ואהרן: ואתכם יהיו איש איש
למטה איש ראש לבית־אבתיו

פ פ ו פ

וידבר קי אשידיכן או קיריוש
פרוש טון מושי איש טין אירימון
טו סיני איש טין טנדא טו טרומא
איש טין מניא טו מינו טו ד
דפטרו צ׳ יש טון כרונו טון ד
דפטרו איש טו אכנלמטוש אפו
טין איי טין איגפטו טו איפי:
שאו מטרישיטי טו קפלי א
אוליש טיש שינגוייש פרוין טו
ישראל איש טיש ייני טוש איש
טושפיטי טון גוניידוטוש מי פ
פשיפויש אונומטא פן אשרניקו
איש טא קפקלאטוש: מכן
אפו יון איקושי כרונו קי אפנו
פאן אופו אוייני שסרטיא איש
טון ישראל נא אנגרפשיטי א

THE PENTATEUCH WITH TARGUM (UPPER MARGIN), SPANISH TRANSLATION (ON THE RIGHT), NEO-GREEK (ON THE LEFT), AND RASHI (LOWER MARGIN) —
CONSTANTINOPLE 1547

(From the Mayer Sulzberger Collection in the Jewish Theological Seminary of America)

חמשה חומשי תורה

ספר בראשית

ראש ערשטי קאפיטל א

בראשית

ראש צווייטי קאפיטל ב

WITZENHAUSEN'S JUDEO-GERMAN VERSION, AMSTERDAM 1679

(In the possession of the Hon. Mayer Sulzberger, Philadelphia) the Jews adopted the expression ' young woman ' or retained the Hebrew word untranslated (' la alma ').

In Judeo-German. We possess a manuscript translation of a part of the Bible in Judeo-German dating from the year 1421. A translation of the Pentateuch in the same dialect was printed at Constance 1543-44 by the baptized Jew Michael Adam, and Elias Levita's rendition of the Psalms appeared at Venice in 1545. The most popular work, constituting to this day in the east of Europe the Bible of the Jewish woman, was the ' Teutsch-Homesh,' also known as the 'Zeenah u-reenah (Go forth, ye women, and see),' by Jacob son of Isaac of Janow, which was printed in Amsterdam in 1649. The first complete Bible in Judeo-German was that of Jekuthiel Blitz (Amsterdam 1676-8), and another version by Joseph Witzenhausen (Amsterdam 1679) was approved by the Council of the Four Lands.

Versions by Samaritans. The Samaritans had an Arabic translation of the Pentateuch by Abu Said (eleventh century) who adapted Saadya's version to the needs of his own people; the Karaites likewise had an Arabic translation of their own, made by a learned contemporary of the Gaon; they also read the Scriptures in a Tataric version, dating from about 1640 (printed in Goslov 1841-2).

Versions by Karaites.

CHAPTER V

THE AGE OF THE REFORMATION. LUTHER AND THE KING JAMES VERSION

The official Bible in Christian Europe throughout the Middle Ages was Jerome's Latin in the West and the Greek in the Byzantine Empire. Vernacular translations, at first mere paraphrases in rhyme or prose and partial, confined to the Psalter, in course of time verbal and complete, arose everywhere. Where

The Eve of the Reformation. the spoken language was akin to Latin, as in Romanic countries, the attempts naturally date from the time when the gulf between the mother-tongue and the daughter dialects widened and the older language was no longer understood by the people; elsewhere the need manifested itself so soon as Christianity had taken root and here and there at the very moment of its introduction. Thus Cyrillus and Methodius, the apostles to the Slavs, are said to have invented for them an alphabet based on the Greek, and are credited with having laid the foundation for the version in the Old-Bulgarian dialect which from

the very beginning was used in the services of the
Orthodox Church. In the Catholic West vernacular
renditions were private undertakings as an aid to the
understanding of the Latin upon which they were
based and often accompanying it in the form of inter-
linears. The Catholic Church, as guardian of the
Scriptures, was rather jealous of the vernacular
Bible; frequently indeed, from the early thirteenth
century downward to the rise of the Reformation,
Bible translating went hand in hand with movements
aimed at breaking down the Church's authority by
the very appeal to the direct Word of God, and was
undertaken in spite of ' the opinion of many clergy
that the mysteries of the Bible should be kept from
the ordinary man.' Venerable monuments of the
early history of Europe's national languages, these
translations are far more important as so many stages
in a religious upheaval, long in preparation, culminating in that revolt of the North which rent the Church
in twain. The first complete French translation dates
from the middle of the thirteenth century; a partial
version in Provençal had preceded it among the followers of Peter Waldus, influencing in turn the
earliest efforts in Italian in the fourteenth century;
the first complete English Bible is associated with the
name of Wycliffe who in the same century led the
attack against the Papacy; versions in German multi-

plied as the Papal authority declined; in the early
fifteenth century John Huss, the Bohemian reformer,
who perfected a vernacular translation for his
countrymen, was burned at the stake.   In all these
centuries, though the Word of God proved its inherent potency with which it found its way to the minds

**The Invention
of Printing.**

and hearts of the people, Bible copies,
multiplied by hand, were costly.   It
required the invention of printing to
spread the vernacular Scriptures among the masses.
The first printed book was the Bible in Latin
(1452-6), and more than a dozen editions of the
German Bible were issued from various presses before
the first edition of the Greek (the Complutensian,
printed in 1517, published in 1520; the Aldine at
Venice, 1518-9) made its appearance.   When on the
10th of December, 1520, Martin Luther signified his
break with Rome by committing to the flames the

**The Printed
Hebrew Bible.**

whole body of the canon law, twenty-
one partial or complete editions of
the Hebrew Scriptures had been
struck off from presses owned by Jews or Christians,
pious wealthy Jews sometimes defraying the costs
(chapter VII), under the editorial care, or at least
with the assistance, of learned Jews.   The most
notable of these editions, opening up the stores of
Jewish exegetical labors, was the first Rabbinic Bible

Incipit prologus sancti Jeronimi presbiteri in parabolas salomonis.

Iungat epistola quos iungit sacerdotium: immo carta non diuidat: quos xpi nectit amor. Cōmentarios in oseam amos: zachariā malachiā: quoq; postis. Scripsissem: si licuisset per ualitudinem. Mittitis solacia sumptuum notarios nros et librarios sustentatis: ut vobis potissimū nrm desudet ingeniū. Et ecce ex latere frequēs turba diuersa poscentiū: quasi aut equū sit me vobis esurientibus alijs laborare: aut in racione dati et accepti: cuiq; preter vos obnox9 sim. Itaq; lōga egrotatione fractus: ne penitus hoc anno reticerē: et apud vos mutus essem: tridui opus nomini vro consecraui: interpretatione videlicet triū salomonis voluminū: masloth qd hebrei parabolas: vulgata editio pūbia vocat: coeleth quē grece ecclesiasten latine cōcionatorē possum9 dicere: sirasirim: qd ĩ linguā nram vertit canticū cāticoꝛ. Fertur et panarettos: ihu filij sirach liber: et ali9 pseudographus: qui sapientia salomonis inscribit. Quoꝝ priorē hebraicum reperi: nō ecclesiasticū ut apud latinos: sed parabolas pnotatū. Cui iūctī erāt ecclesiastes et canticū canticoꝝ: ut similitudinē salomonis nō solū numero libroꝝ: sed etiā materiaꝝ genere coequaret. Secūdus apud hebreos nusꝗ; est: quia et ipse stilus grecam eloquentiā redolet: et nōnulli scriptorū veterū hūc esse iudei filonis affirmant. Sicud ergo iudith et thobie et machabeoꝝ libros: legit quidē eos ecclia: sed inter canoicas scripturas nō recipit: sic et hec duo volumina legat ad edificatione plebis: nō ad auctoritatem ecclesiasticoꝝ dogmatū cōfirmandam.

Si cui sane septuaginta interpretum magis editio placet: habet eā a nobis olim emēdatā. Neq; enī noua sic cudim9: ut vetera destruam9. Et tamē cū diligentissime legerit: sciat magis nra scripta intelligi: que nō in terciū vas transfusa coacuerit: sed statim de prelo purissime̅ mēdata testi: suū saporē seruauerit. Incipit parabole salomonis.

Parabole salomonis filij dauid regis isrl: ad sciendā sapientiā et disciplinā: ad intelligendā verba prudentie et suscipiendā eruditionē doctrine: iustitiā et iudiciū et equitatē: ut detur paruulis astucia: et adolescenti scientia et intellectus. Audiens sapiēs sapiētior erit: et intelligens gubernacla possidebit. Aniaduertet parabolam et interpretationē: verba sapientiū et enigmata eoꝝ. Timor dūi principiū sapientie. Sapientiam atꝗ; doctrinam stulti despiciūt. Audi fili mi disciplinā pris tui et ne dimittas legem mris tue: ut addatur gracia capiti tuo: et torques collo tuo. Fili mi si te lactauerint peccatores: ne acquiescas eis. Si dixerint veni nobiscū insidiemur sāguini: abscondam9 tediculas cōtra insontem frustra: deglutiam9 eū sicut infernus viuentem et integrum: quasi descendentē in lacū: omnē preciosā substantiā reperiem9: implebim9 domus nras spolijs: sortem mitte nobiscum: marsupiū sit unum omniū nrm: fili mi ne ambules cū eis. Prohibe pedem tuū a semitis eoꝝ. Pedes eni̅ illoꝝ ad malū currūt: et festinant ut effundant sāguinem. Frustra autem iacit rete ante oculos pēnatoꝝ. Ipi qꝗ; contra sanguinē suū insidiantur: et

FIRST RABBINIC BIBLE, VENICE 1516–7

With Targum and Kimhi's Commentary.

(In the possession of the Hon. Mayer Sulzberger, Philadelphia)

issued in Venice (1516-7) by Felix Pratensis, a convert to Christianity, and dedicated to Pope Leo X;
an improved and much enlarged edition followed in
1524-5 including the Masorah revised and compiled
by Jacob son of Haim Ibn Adonijah, who subsequently likewise embraced Christianity. Thus the
way was paved for the newer Bible learning in which
Christian scholars, at first timidly and largely in
dependence upon Jewish predecessors, then with
greater originality and with increased facilities, were
to exercise themselves, and Bible translating was
placed on a surer foundation by a return to the original fountain-head.

In the early sixteenth century a Catholic editor
of the Vulgate complains that the Jews make light of
Translations based on the Original. the Church translation and urge upon
the head of the Church of Rome the
need of a new rendition. Somewhat
earlier, toward the end of the fifteenth
century, a German translator of the Vulgate declares
it as his purpose that every intelligent layman may
know how to answer the ' evil-minded Jews.' Of the
In Latin. new Latin translations based on the original we may single out those by Sanctes
Pagninus (1541), Sebastian Münster (1534-5), Leo
Juda (Zwingli's collaborator; he was assisted by a
baptized Jew) and his associates (1543), Chateillon

(who also translated the Bible into French, 1551),
Immanuel Tremellius, a baptized Jew, with whom
was associated his son-in-law du Jon (1579). All
of these, more or less felicitously executed, were
learned productions, and they proved of great assistance to those whose familiarity with the original
tongues, notably the Hebrew, was rather modest.
Münster's rendition indirectly influenced the King
James Version. The use of Latin explains itself
only from its being the language of the learned,
continued beyond the century of the Reformation.
But the very essence of the revolt against Rome consisted in the breaking up of the international Church-
empire and in the rise of the independent state-nation-
alities; and wherever the reformatory movement took
root, the placing of the Bible within the comprehension of the laity by means of vernacular renditions
followed of necessity. The Vulgate and the translations derived from it were to be banished; new
translations based upon the original took their place.

Foremost among the Protestant translations,
monuments at once of the new piety and the national
Luther's cultures with which they became in-
Translation. terwoven, are Luther's German Bible
on the continent of Europe and the
various attempts in England culminating in the
Authorized Version of 1611. Luther based his trans-

lation upon the original, using the Brescia edition of
1494; his knowledge of Hebrew and Aramaic, however, was but moderate. Naturally he made use of
commentaries, chiefly those of Nicholas Lyranus,
which, as was pointed out above (chapter IV), went
back to Rashi, and also of earlier translations. The
work proceeded slowly, the Book of Job in particular
baffling his ingenuity, and days were sometimes spent
over a few verses. For the Book of Leviticus he had
several sheep killed, and a butcher of the town named
to him in German the various parts of the animal.
The work was completed in 1530, and the first complete edition of Luther's version appeared in 1534.
The avowed aim of the translator was to serve the
needs of the common people; he therefore strove to
make his rendition clear and intelligible, without,
however, destroying the coloring of the original.
Ten editions issued during Luther's lifetime testify
to the popularity of the work which, while not free
from faults and here and there marred by straining
a doctrinal point in a spirit of polemics, secured a
permanent hold on the German nation, and largely
promoted the development of the German language
and literature. With the spread of Lutheranism beyond the confines of Germany, Luther's version
became the basis of the translations used in Denmark,
Sweden, Norway, and Holland.

Luther's influence is also clearly perceptible in the first printed English Bible, the work of William Tyndale. The pupil of Erasmus at Cambridge, upon discovering that ' there was no place in all England '

Tyndale. to execute a translation of the Scriptures into English, chose to exile himself to Germany, where he made ample use of the version by the German reformer. His translation of the Pentateuch was printed in 1530; a strongly controversial tone marked the annotations, which, in part at least, were derived from Luther. In 1531 followed the Book of Jonah. Tyndale continued to be busy with revisions of his previous efforts and with preparing for print other parts of the Scriptures. Imprisoned in Belgium at the instigation of his enemies, he touchingly asked for warmer clothing, but also for a Hebrew Bible, grammar, and dictionary; on the sixth of October, 1536, he died a martyr to the cause of the English Bible, and his last words at the stake were a prayer that God might open the king of England's eyes. The first complete translation of

Coverdale. the Bible into English, printed in 1535-6, was dedicated to the king (Henry VIII); it was the work of Miles Coverdale, and was undertaken at the bidding of Thomas Cromwell. Coverdale lacked originality, his sources being Luther, Tyndale, and the Swiss-German version by Zwingli and Leo

Juda; but his work won the approbation of the throne, and the Bible in English circulated freely among the people despite the hostility of the bishops. Fresh translations, which were really revisions, followed quickly. In 1537 appeared what is

Matthew's Bible. known as Matthew's Bible, based chiefly upon Tyndale's published and manuscript efforts; it was sold in England by leave of the king and the Archbishop of Canterbury. A new revision by Coverdale, with the aid of Münster's Latin version, followed in 1539-41 (the Great Bible), and copies of it were set up in every church.

The Great Bible. The people flocked to the churches, disdaining the sermons of the preachers, but listening to the Word of God itself read by some one, in disregard of the order of divine service, to a crowd of worshippers, and we hear of an ecclesiastic making complaint that ' diverse wilful and unlearned persons inconsiderately and indiscreetly read the English Scriptures, especially and chiefly at the time of divine service, yea in the time and declaration of the word of God.' The spirit of the complaint is that which held the common people in tutelage; in the eagerness of the people who would convert the churches into reading conventicles and meeting-houses there was brought to new life the spirit of Judea and its synagogues.

The reaction which set in under Mary, with Cranmer and Rogers burnt at the stake, drove the reformers to the continent. There the Puritan followers of John Knox separated from the moderate section and withdrew to Geneva, the home of Calvin, the Swiss reformer, and of Beza, the most prominent

The Geneva Bible. biblical scholar of the day. A new English translation was the result, the work of Whittingham and a group of kindred spirits, who based themselves on the Great Bible, introducing at the same time many alterations which were marked by a closer approximation to the Hebrew. The edition, known as the Geneva or Breeches Bible (Genesis 2. 7 read: They sewed fig-leaves together and made themselves breeches; so already Wycliffe), appeared in 1557-60. It at once became popular (between 1560 and the outbreak of Civil War in England no less than 160 editions were struck off), supplanting in the private homes of the people the Great Bible, an unwieldy folio volume used in the churches. It is the first English Bible with verse numeration. It had marginal notes, Calvinist in tone, but generally free from offensive asperity. Its influence on the King James Version was marked.

With the restoration of Protestantism under Elizabeth steps were taken for a new revision which might be acceptable for public service. The Great Bible had been discredited by the Genevan effort; yet the latter was too much identified with a particular party in the Church to serve the purpose. In the year 1562 Archbishop Parker, a man of great learning, invited a company of divines, who for the most part were bishops (hence the name Bishops' Bible), to undertake the task. Each of the collaborators was assigned

The Bishops' Bible. a portion of the Scriptures, the Archbishop reserving for himself the work of editing the whole and seeing it through the press. The Bishops' Bible was printed in 1568 and at once introduced in the churches. It failed, however, to supersede the Geneva version. There was too much unevenness in the new revision, the several revisers working separately and without consultation with their fellow-workers. Thus upon the

The King James Version. accession of James I a fresh undertaking was set on foot resulting in the King James Version of 1611. A scheme was drawn up in 1604 by the king himself who selected in person the revisers from both the ritualist and puritan parties of the Church.

The King's Instructions. The most important instructions were the following:

'The ordinary Bible read in the church, commonly called "the Bishops' Bible," to be followed, and as little altered as the truth of the original will permit.

The old ecclesiastical words to be kept.

No marginal notes at all to be affixed, but only for the explanation of Hebrew . . . words.

Every particular man of each company to take the same chapter or chapters, and having translated or amended them severally by himself, where he thinketh good, all to meet together, confer what they have done, and agree for their parts what shall stand.'

As each company finished one book, they were to send it to the other companies for their careful consideration. Where doubts prevailed as to any passage of special obscurity, letters were to be sent to ' any learned man in the land ' for his judgment. Finally, ' three or four of the most ancient and grave divines in either of the universities, not employed in translating,' were to be 'overseers of the translations.' In 1607 the task was taken in hand. One group worked in Westminster at Genesis—II Kings; another, at Oxford, revised Isaiah—Malachi; two, at Cambridge, were busy with I Chronicles—Ecclesiastes and the Apocrypha. The work on the entire body of the Church Scriptures was accomplished in the short time of two years and nine months, the last nine months being taken up by a final revision entrusted to a committee consisting of two members from each center, the total number of revisers being

from forty-eight to fifty. The quaint preface to the
1611 edition contains interesting information on the
manner in which the revisers executed their task.
' Matters of such weight and consequence,' they
write, ' are to be speeded with maturity; for in a
business of moment a man feareth not the blame of

**From the
Preface to
the King
James
Version.**

convenient slackness. Neither did we
think much to consult translators or
commentators, Chaldee, Hebrew, Syrian,
Greek, or Latin; no, nor the Spanish
[1569 and 1602], French [1587-8],
Italian [1607], or Dutch [the German of
Luther]; neither did we disdain to revise that which
we had done, and to bring back to the anvil that which
we had hammered; but having and using as great
helps as were needful, and fearing no reproach for
slowness, nor coveting praise for expedition, we have
at length, through the good hand of the Lord upon
us, brought the work to that pass that you see.'
Among the ' great helps ' was the Geneva Bible.
The revisers in particular defend two important
points. The first touches the margin from which
indeed all comments, not needed for the understanding of the text and in the previous efforts marred by
a controversial spirit, were sedulously ruled out.
' Some peradventure,' they say, ' would have no
variety of senses to be set in the margin, lest the

6

authority of the Scriptures for deciding of contro-
versies by that show of uncertainty should somewhat
be shaken.   But we hold their judgment not to be so
sound in this point. . . .   It hath pleased God in his
Divine Providence, here and there to scatter words
and sentences of that difficulty and doubtfulness, not
in doctrinal points that concern salvation (for in such
it hath been vouched that the Scriptures are plain),
but in matters of less moment, that fearfulness would
better beseem us than confidence. . . .   There be
many words in the Scriptures, which be never found
there but once (having neither brother nor neighbor,
as the Hebrews speak), so that we cannot be holpen
by conference of places.   Again, there be many rare
names of certain birds, beasts, and precious stones,
etc., concerning which the Hebrews themselves are
so divided among themselves for judgment, that they
may seem to have defined this or that, rather because
they would say something, than because they were
sure of that which they said, as St. Jerome somewhere
saith of the Septuagint.   Now in such a case doth not
a margin do well to admonish the reader to seek further, and not to conclude or dogmatize upon this or
that peremptorily?   For as it is a fault of incredulity,
to doubt of those things that are evident; so to deter-
mine of those things as the Spirit of God hath left
(even in the judgment of the judicious) questionable,

can be no less than presumption.' The other point concerns the avowed lack of uniformity in rendering words of the original text. ' That we should express the same notion in the same particular word; as for example, if we translate the Hebrew . . . word once by *purpose,* never to call it *intent;* if one where *journeying,* never *travelling;* if one where *think,* never *suppose;* if one where *pain,* never *ache;* if one where *joy,* never *gladness,* etc., thus to mince the matter, we thought to savor more of curiosity than wisdom, and that rather it would breed scorn in the atheist, than bring profit to the godly reader.'

When the revision left the press, it was attacked by Doctor Hugh Broughton, a biblical scholar of **The Work Criticised.** great eminence and erudition, who had been omitted from the list of revisers on account of his violent and impracticable disposition, and whose disappointment vented itself in a very hostile criticism of the new version. Despite all cavilling, it became the official version of the Anglican Church; though there is no record of an official decree ordaining its use in the service, it was and is still spoken of as the Authorized Version; after half a century it outdistanced the Geneva Bible in popularity, taking its place as the undisputed Bible of the English nation. Its production fell upon a period when, as at no other time, the standard of literary taste, under the influence of such masters as Spenser, Sidney, Hooker, Marlowe, and Shakespeare, was at its highest. It has an inimitable charm and rhythm ; the coloring of the original is not obliterated,

Its Matchless Diction.   and yet examples abound of idiomatic renditions reproducing the thought in an admirable manner. It ranks as a classic in English literature, and has exercised a potent influence upon writers of English to this day. A venerable document of a great literary and religious period, after three centuries of unquestioned sway, it was found capable of improvement on the side of interpretation and in some of its vocabulary and phraseology which are not quite intelligible to readers acquainted with modern English only ; but all

A Basis for all Future Revisions.   attempts at a fresh revision have based themselves upon it as a starting-point. When modern revisers have changed its matchless diction where no difference of meaning was involved, they have erred in their zeal. Practical as the object of all Bible translations must be, the King James Version, in which so many earlier efforts have deposited their happiest and best, has pointed out the way how with accuracy of rendition there must go elegance of style, and how a translation of the Scriptures must aim at rivalling the stately diction of the original.

CHAPTER VI

MODERN TRANSLATIONS BY JEWS AND CHRISTIANS

The 'great helps' which were available when the King James Version was produced were largely increased as the centuries rolled on. The study of Arabic was begun in Europe almost simultaneously with that of Hebrew, and notable progress was achieved early. At Oxford the chair of Arabic was worthily occupied by Edward Pococke from 1636 to 1691. Syriac studies were propagated in the seventeenth century by Assemani and others, while Ludolf in 1661 opened up a knowledge of Ethiopic. The greatest undertaking of the seventeenth century was the London Polyglot edited by Brian Walton with the assistance of many scholars (1655-57), which superseded earlier efforts by its wealth of contents; the Oriental versions invited a comparative study of the languages in which they were composed; a still greater help proved the appended dictionary of seven Oriental tongues, the

Progress of Biblical Studies after 1611: Among Christians.

stupendous work of Edmund Castle which cost him
his eye-sight and the bulk of his private fortune.
European scholars, led by de Dieu and others, re-
discovered the affinity of the Semitic dialects which
had long before been set forth by the Jewish grammarians of the first three centuries of the second
millennium.   English scholars of the seventeenth
century compiled two collections of biblical commentaries by Christian scholars who combined with the
newer learning a mastery of rabbinic lore.   The
received Hebrew text was criticised as faulty by
Cappellus (1624) and Morinus (1669) and just as
stubbornly defended by Buxtorf the younger (1648,
1662).   Buxtorf's work was carried on somewhat
pedantically by Alting in Holland (1654) and Danz
in Germany (1696) who made light of comparative
grammar; but the eighteenth century witnessed a
revival of the method by which the other Semitic
dialects, chiefly the Arabic, were drawn upon for an
elucidation of the Hebrew language, both in structure and vocabulary.   Its most illustrious exponent
was Albert Schultens in Holland (1686-1750) who,
however, in his zeal overshot the mark.   In Germany,
the three Michaelis did creditable work through
textual editions and commentaries, marking the
transition from pietistic orthodoxy to rationalism.
Towards the end of the century Carsten Niebuhr

brought home with him from a journey to the Orient
more accurate and complete copies of the Achaemen-
ian inscriptions at Persepolis, and thus laid the foundation for a decipherment of the Assyrian wedge-
shaped script; excavations of the ancient mounds in
the Tigris-Euphrates valley, carried on successively
in the nineteenth century, brought to light the Assyro-
Babylonian as a new, hitherto unknown, Semitic
tongue, and laid bare a vast literature which proved
of great value for a knowledge of ancient Oriental
civilization and history in biblical times. While
Kennicott in England (1776-80) and de Rossi in
Italy (1784-88) published their scholarly results of
the collation of hundreds of manuscripts of the
Hebrew Scriptures, Lowth translated and expounded
Isaiah, freely admitting that the prophets spoke pri-
marily to the men of their own time. Equally famous
is his treatise on the sacred poetry of the Hebrews
(1753), which, together with Herder's essay on the
same subject (1782), paved the way for the study of
the Bible as literature. Herder's intuitive conception
of a people's literature as rooted in the folk soul and
in a distinct civilization was systematized in profes-
sorial language by Eichhorn who emphasized that
the Hebrew Scriptures were to be understood in
their Oriental setting; he also independently hit upon
the conjecture, advanced some time previously by

Jean Astruc, that the Pentateuch was composed of a number of parallel ' documents.'   At the turn of the century we find Rosenmüller at Leipzig compiling a voluminous commentary on the Bible, and Gesenius at Halle in a sober and painstaking manner building up the science of Hebrew grammar and lexicography. Far more original was Gesenius' pugnacious rival Ewald, who as grammarian, translator, and historian became the guide of the modern school of Bible students.   Dillmann, who, like a second Ludolf, was master of Ethiopic lore, and who will be remembered as one of the greatest commentators of the nineteenth century, Wellhausen, who revolutionized the study of biblical history, and Nöldeke, the greatest Orientalist of our age, all acknowledge their indebtedness to Ewald.   Of a more conservative bent of mind was Franz Delitzsch, the erudite student of rabbinic literature, excelling alike in mastery of detail and in ripe independent judgment.   Biblical learning has since made stupendous progress.   The Bible lands have been explored, described, and surveyed ; excavations everywhere bring to light undreamt-of finds shedding light on the remote past in which the sacred writers lived ; the languages and fortunes of many races mentioned in the Bible have been thoroughly studied ; a critical method has been applied to the ancient records, biblical and non-biblical. Two new sciences, that of comparative religion and that of comparative literature, are assisting in the clarification of many points scarcely touched upon in older commentaries. In the modern commentary the net result of all these multifarious branches of biblical study is deposited; it is to be regretted, however, that the commentary of the very latest sort is more concerned with all the by-work of criticism than with verbal interpretation. Compared with the master-builders of half a century ago, the average Bible commentator of to-day has a very inadequate knowledge of Hebrew, knows still less of later Hebrew, and obtains his information concerning the versions from second-hand sources. The text of the original is being freely tampered with in a manner which would be laughed at in the field of classical studies. Moreover, it cannot be denied that there is an undercurrent of hostility to things Hebrew and a lack of sympathy with the Hebrew Scriptures. All biblical scholars are naturally interested in the literature of the Apocrypha and Pseudepigrapha, and here again great achievements have been made and new texts brought to light. Serious Christian scholars are fully cognizant of the fact that the Pentateuch requires for its elucidation a knowledge of the rabbinical halakah.

Among the Jews, biblical learning in the centuries that followed the expulsion from Spain remained at a standstill. With the destruction of the Jewish center in the land where great achievements had been accomplished, the Jewish scholars lost contact with the Arabic, a knowledge of which proved so fruitful in the hands of Christian Hebraists. Moreover, the catastrophe itself produced a depression of the spirit which inclined the mind to allegorical and mystical interpretation, and prevented deep researches in philology. In Italy and in free Holland secular learning was within the reach of the Jew: Azariah dei Rossi in the sixteenth century, who translated the Epistle of Aristeas into Hebrew and revived interest in the long forgotten Alexandrian version, stood like an isolated peak, and was far in advance of his time, and Manasseh ben Israel in the seventeenth century, who appealed to Cromwell for the re-admission of his co-religionists into England, was in touch with the Dutch school of Christian Hebraists, and utilised his wide learning in the effort to straighten out biblical difficulties. His erudite work, the *Conciliador,* written in Spanish, has been translated into Latin, Italian, and English. From the Levant and Italy hailed the two students of the Masorah, a difficult and abstruse subject which elsewhere was left severely alone: Menahem Lonzano

(marginal note:) **Among Jews.**

(1618) and Solomon Jedidiah Norzi (1626). In 1628 a Jew of Posen, Isaac Levita, anticipated Alting's philosophical treatment of Hebrew grammar, and in the early eighteenth century Solomon Hanau in Germany, who sustained himself as an elementary teacher travelling from place to place, propounded novel theories of vowel development in Hebrew. For the most part the best minds of Germany and Poland exercised themselves in the casuistry of the Talmud and the codes or were immersed in mysticism. Once more the Talmud overshadowed the Bible, and the most that was done in the exposition of the Scriptures consisted in writing long-winded supercommentaries. The German Jews of the eighteenth century were, with a few exceptions, devoid of secular education; the instruction of the youth was in the hands of teachers from the East to whom a Hebrew grammar was an impious book. In **The Second** this environment grew up the man to **Return to** whom it fell to effect the second return **the Bible.** to the Bible, which paved the way for the Jewish renaissance—a revolution of Jewish thought and life penetrating the darkest corners of the East and creating multitudinous problems of adjustment which to the present day occupy the minds of Jewish leaders.

Moses Mendelssohn, the popularizer of Wolffian philosophy and the man of letters who enjoyed the friendship of Lessing and his circle, opened a new epoch through his translation into High German of biblical books, in particular of the Pentateuch. Its effect upon his co-religionists was twofold. It served **Mendelssohn and his School.** as a text-book for acquiring the language of the educated, which led naturally to familiarity with the German literature and German culture. Then again inwardly it wrought a change by luring away the youth from the narrower occupation with codes and casuistry to the wider field of biblical interpretation and to the appreciation of the Scriptures as literature demanding and creating an aesthetic taste. The translation was accompanied by a commentary in Hebrew, rational and grammatical, for which the best of the older commentators were excerpted and in part the results of Christian research were utilized; while Mendelssohn himself wrote a considerable portion thereof, the more difficult books were expounded by his collaborators, notably the grammarian Solomon Dubno and the poet Hartwig Wessely. Though the work won the approbation of the Berlin rabbinate, it was put under the ban by the spiritual leaders of Altona, Fürth, and Frankfort-on-the-Main; the uncompromising Moses Sofer, who died in 1839, admonished his children to refrain from reading Mendelssohn's writings. The friends and disciples of the philosopher, of whom the best known is David Friedländer (1750-1834), completed the work of translation and exposition for the rest of the Bible. The coterie of scholars who handled the Hebrew language with the skill of the best medieval writers came to be known as the Biurists, from the word Biur (interpretation) by which the commentary was designated. What characterizes them is a sober rationalism, which, however, lacked the solid foundation of historical perspective and critical acumen. To the Mendelssohnian era belongs Judah Loeb Benseeb (died in 1811), the grammarian and lexicographer; Ignaz Jeitteles (1773-1838), the author of a very imperfect grammar of the Aramaic; and Solomon Pappenheim (1740-1814), the writer on Hebrew synonymics. Under the spell of the sage of Berlin stood likewise the fine grammarian and student of the Masorah Wolf Heidenheim (1757-1832). The nineteenth century saw the rise of the scientific school, headed by Solomon Judah Rapoport (1790-1867) and Leopold Zunz (1794-1886). Obscure periods in Jewish history and large important portions of Jewish

The Biurists.

Rise of the Scientific School.

literature were made the subject of painstaking inves-
tigations characterized by vast erudition as well as
by the application of the critical method.   Zunz made
noteworthy contributions to biblical criticism; the
The Zunz German translation of the Bible, with
Bible. which his name is associated, was largely
the work of Arnheim, Fürst, and Sachs,
and served a practical need (1837-8).   In general it
may be said that, with notable exceptions, the scholars
who followed Zunz's lead in the building up of the
science of Judaism left the Bible severely alone.
Geiger. Abraham Geiger (1810-1874), who early
in life came under the influence of Heidenheim, had the sagacity to recognize that the structure
which these men were rearing would be incomplete
unless a reverential but at the same time critical study
of the Bible were included, and that, so long as Jewish scholars, bent upon discoveries in new soil, dis-
dained exploring the mines of the old biblical field,
the Christian hegemony in Bible work would remain
in force.   In an epoch-making work, by which biblical scholars of the subsequent generation, both among
Jews and Christians, were profoundly stimulated,
Geiger sought to trace the inner history of the original text and the ancient versions as it kept pace with
the progress of religious ideas in Judaism.   The

arguments in detail have proved capable of correction in the light of newer finds and knowledge, but the main thesis of the book remains unshaken. Zechariah Frankel (1801-1875), the first head of the Breslau Rabbinical Seminary, made the Alexandrian version the subject of fruitful studies, and his younger colleague, the far-famed historian of the Jewish people, Heinrich Graetz (1817-1891), made noteworthy contributions to biblical science. It will suffice to single out his works on the Song of Songs and Ecclesiastes (1871) and his two volumes on the Psalter (1882-3). It must be owned that in these works, as well as in his 'Emendations' posthumously published by Bacher (1892-3), he shows an all too facile method of dealing with the received text. In Italy, at the beginning of the nineteenth century, Isaac Samuel Reggio (1784-1855) was the author of an Italian translation of the Pentateuch accompanied by a Hebrew commentary (Vienna 1821), both still largely under the influence of the Mendelssohnian school. From him proceeded the impetus to the foundation of the Rabbinical School at Padua; to its head, **Luzzatto.** Samuel David Luzzatto (1800-1865), unquestionably belongs the first rank among modern Jewish students of the Bible. It may be said of him that he raised biblical studies among the Jews to

the dignity of a specialty, requiring a man's whole
time and energy and pursued as a profession. Scion
of an ancient family from which had sprung many
erudite scholars, he possessed a wide range of Jewish
and secular knowledge, and wrote Hebrew with masterly efficiency. He had access to rare manuscript
treasures, and was at home in the medieval literature
of the best Jewish grammarians and commentators.
His study of Onkelos was epoch-making, and stimulated Geiger's researches; he wrote a Hebrew grammar in Italian on modern lines; his grammar of the
biblical (and talmudic) Aramaic elicited the praises
of Nöldeke; his commentary on Isaiah and his shorter
comments on other books of the Bible show the painstaking scholar and judicious critic; his translations
of several biblical books into Italian, notably of Job
(1853), Isaiah (1855), and the Pentateuch (1871-6),
were based on a thorough acquaintance with Hebrew
in all its stages, and bore witness to a deep love for
Judaism and the monuments of the past. He was a
bitter foe of the Northern innovations which meant
to him the surrender of Judaism to the spirit of Hel-
lenism, and he was equally severe on Ibn Ezra and
Maimonides for their compromise with the alien
spirit. While Luzzatto with all his battling against
the forces of disintegration remained the objective
student who sought the truth and knew how to keep

apart the plain meaning of the Scriptures scientifically ascertained and the later outgrowth of rabbinic
Samson Raphael Hirsch. interpretation, Samson Raphael Hirsch (1808-1888), the protagonist of orthodoxy in the West, subordinated in his German Pentateuch (1867) the Bible word to tradition; on more original lines worked in the East Meir Leibush Malbim (1809-1879), who sought
Malbim. to prove by fine observations of the idiom of the Scriptures how the tradition of the rabbis was rooted in the biblical word. On similar lines, in our own days, D. Hoffmann (1843—), who successfully combated Wellhausen on his own ground (1904), produced a notable commentary on Leviticus (1905-6) and on Deuteronomy (the first part, 1913). Luzzatto and Malbim were drawn upon half a century ago by the learned Franz Delitzsch; to-day it is gratifying to note the frequency with which Christian commentators make
Ehrlich. mention of a living Jewish Bible student, Arnold B. Ehrlich, an American by long residence in this country. His great work on the Bible, first published in Hebrew, which he masterfully handles, and latterly, in much enlarged form, in German (seven volumes, 1908-14; the book of Psalms is dealt with in a separate volume which appeared in 1905), though marred by irrelevant

7

attacks on time-hallowed tradition and by the confident spirit with which untenable positions are advanced, is nevertheless replete with solid and original observations, testifying to a profound insight into Hebrew idiom.

With the entry of the Jew into modern civilization, Bible translations into various European languages **Translations into Various European Languages.** became a necessity. Foremost stands the French Bible (1831-51), the work of the erudite S. Cahen, which was enriched by many contributions from the pen of Solomon Munk (1803-67) and Leopold Dukes. Lazare Wogue is the author of another French version (incomplete; the Pentateuch appeared 1860-9), which was largely the basis of a popular version by members of the rabbinate in France, under the direction of Zadoc Kahn the chief rabbi (1899-1906). In Germany the translations by Philippson (1839-56), Herxheimer (1840-8), and Fürst (1874) showed progress. In Holland, a Dutch translation by S. I. Mulder was printed between 1826 and 1838 (incomplete); in 1901 the Pentateuch was rendered afresh into Dutch by A. S. Onderwijser. In Italy, Luzzatto's pupils produced a complete Italian version (1868-75). The Pentateuch and the Psalter have been done into Russian by L. I. Mandelstamm (1862, 1864). A Hungarian

translation was prepared from materials supplied by
Immanuel Löw, Gyula Fischer, and other rabbis, by
an editorial committee consisting of Vilmos Bacher,
Jozsef Banoczi, and Samuel Krauss; it was issued
in 1898-1907 by the Jewish Hungarian Literary

**Translations
into English.**
Society. In England Isaac Delgado,
'teacher of the Hebrew Language,'
printed in 1789 a new English translation of the Pentateuch in the form of corrections of 'the present translation [*i. e.,* the King
James Version] wherever it deviates from the genu-
ine sense of the Hebrew expressions, or where it
renders obscure the meaning of the text, or, lastly,
when it occasions a seeming contradiction,' dedi-
cating his work to Dr. Shute Barrington, Lord
Bishop of Salisbury. Selig Newman published in
1839 his *Emendations of the Authorized Version,*
and the learned Kalisch wrote a valuable commentary
in English on Exodus (1855), Genesis (1858), and
Leviticus (1867-72). Benisch gave Anglo-Jewry a
complete translation of the Scriptures, which, while
in the legal portions of the Pentateuch it faithfully reproduced Jewish opinion, was intended otherwise to be an impartial product; it appeared in
1851-6. Michael Friedländer, the translator of
Maimonides' *Guide of the Perplexed,* is responsible
for another translation which represents the Author-

ized Version of the Anglican Church slightly retouched (1884).   In America, in the city of Philadelphia, where the first Hebrew Bible (1814) was
Leeser's Bible. printed in this hemisphere, Isaac Leeser
issued in 1853 a complete version of the
Hebrew Scriptures in English, which for
more than half a century has held its place in American and English synagogues.   Leeser based himself
in style upon the King James Version, ' which for
simplicity cannot be surpassed '; but the changes
introduced by him are so many and so great that his
translation may lay claim to being an independent
work.   A specialist in Hebrew philology he certainly
was not, nor did he consider himself such; but he
made good use of the various German translations
by Jews in the preceding eighty years, and he is much
dependent upon the Biurists, Zunz, and the notes in
Philippson's Bible.

The Anglican Revised Version. While thus Jewish scholars, for the
distinct needs of the Synagogue, were
applying themselves to a revision of the
venerable version in use by the Anglican
Church, improved versions of Exodus,
Isaiah, Jeremiah, Ezekiel, Jonah, Zechariah, Lamentations, and Daniel were attempted by Lowth (1778),
Hopkins (1784), Blayney (1784), Newcome (1788),
Wintle (1792), and Benjoin (1796).   At the begin-

ning of the nineteenth century several complete translations appeared.   But all these were private undertakings.   Definite steps to secure a new English
Bible for use by the Church of England, which,
while basing itself upon the translation of 1611,
was to embody the results of modern investigation,
were not taken until 1870.   It was issued from
the press in 1885.   A volume containing the Apocrypha appeared in 1895.   The work of revision
was distributed among two companies, one taking
over the Apocrypha.   In each company sat scholars and divines of renown from the Church of
England and the dissenting Churches.   Among them
were Payne Smith, the Syriac scholar; Cheyne,
Davidson, and Driver, experts in matters of interpretation; Field, a master of the Greek versions; the
Orientalist Sayce; the Arabist W. Robertson Smith;
and for questions affecting the Hebrew text Christian David Ginsburg, born a Jew, who with Frens-
dorff, the Jewish school director at Hanover, and S.
Baer, the Rhenish teacher in an elementary Jewish
school, divided the honors of masoretic lore in the
nineteenth century.   They did their work in 792
days in a space of fourteen years.   Two further companies were at work in America, and there were con-
stant exchanges of discussion between England and
this country.   The method of work is described by

the English Company in the following words: ' In the first Revision it was the practice for the Secretary to read over each verse, first in the original and then in the Authorized Version: the proposals for change were then taken; first those communicated in writing by absent members, and next those made by the members present. Each proposal was moved, and if seconded was discussed and voted upon; the decision in the first Revision being by a majority only. If a proposal met with no seconder, it was not discussed but allowed to drop. In the Second Revision, the Secretary read out in order the changes which had been made at the first Revision; if these were unchallenged they were allowed to remain, otherwise they were put to the vote and affirmed or rejected according as they were or were not supported by the requisite majority of two-thirds. In the second Revision new propositions could only be made by special permission of the Company, and discussion was limited, as far as possible, to exceptional cases. In the final review, which was in reality the completion of the second Revision, the Company employed themselves in making a general survey of what they had done, deciding finally upon reserved points, harmonizing inconsistencies, smoothing down roughnesses, removing unnecessary changes, and generally giving finish and completeness to their work. Everything in this final survey was decided by a vote of a majority of two-thirds.' They wisely refrained from altering the received Hebrew text, although here and there they followed in the footsteps of the older version in giving room to a tacit change. The merits of the Revised Version, as it has come to be called, rest chiefly upon changes of interpretation in which ample use was made of the progress of biblical science which I have attempted to sketch above. So far as the language is concerned, they endeavored to retain that of the version of 1611; where its wording had to be changed because of an altered meaning which had to be adopted, care was taken that the diction was on a level with the older Elizabethan and Jacobean English. It was a bold undertaking to attempt to write in the Victorian age the English of three centuries ago; but in the main, and despite the cavilling of critics, they succeeded. Archaic expressions were changed into less obsolete phraseology, likewise borrowed from past models. The revision was assailed most bitterly by Dean Burgon in a series of articles, learned but extravagant and intemperate. Nevertheless the Revised Version has steadily gained ground. The American edition of the Revised Version, printed by Thomas Nelson & Sons (1900-01), embodies the changes proposed by the American companies and rejected by their English fellow-workers. A questionable innovation on the part of the American editors was the substitution of Jehovah for ' LORD ' to express the tetragrammaton.

Less far-reaching was the revision of Luther's version undertaken by a commission of theologians belonging to the various factions of the Lutheran Church in Germany. A resolution favoring the project was carried at the Church Conference of Eisenach in 1861 and 1863. The first draft (' Probebibel ') was printed in 1883, the **The German Revision. Private Undertakings.** work of revision was brought to a conclusion at the Conference of Halle in 1890 and was issued in final form in 1892. It was at once circulated by the Württemberg Bible Society, while in Northern Germany it has met with a lukewarm reception. Of a private character and with the avowed purpose of bringing to the notice of the educated laity the results of the newer criticism were the undertakings by Eduard Reuss, first in French (1874-81) and then in German (posthumously published in 1892-4), and by Emil Kautzsch (with the assistance of a number of scholars ; first edition 1890-4 ; third edition 1909-12). Both are accompanied by notes and furnished with introductions ; in point of originality and taste Reuss's work is the superior product. On a par with Kautzsch's Bible stands the Dutch version by Kuenen,

Hooykas, Kosters, and Oort (1899-1901), which embodies many deviations from the received Hebrew text. The Variorum Bible, edited by Cheyne and Driver (1876, third edition 1888), gives, under the text of the King James Version, improved renderings and readings. We are further indebted to these two scholars for fresh translations of parts of the Scriptures which are distinguished by learning and elegance of style.

With the exodus of Jews from the east of Europe to the American continent, which began in 1881, and

The New Translation published by the Jewish Publication Society of America. the gradual shifting of the Jewish center to this hemisphere making for the largest aggregate of English-speaking Jews in the world, the need of a new English version of the Bible for use in synagogue, home, and school was bound to make itself felt. Leeser's noble translation was there, but a work resting in the main upon the German efforts of the concluding decades of the eighteenth and the earlier period of the nineteenth century was clearly inadequate at the end of the century when noteworthy contributions to biblical learning had been made by Jews and Christians. The project was conceived at the second biennial convention (1892) of the Jewish Publication Society of America (organized in 1888).

The plan, as worked out by a sub-committee in 1893 and adopted in 1894, called for a revision based on Leeser. By 1896 a Revision Committee consisting of a number of Jewish scholars in America and England, each member undertaking a separate book, was at work, and their labors were to be passed on by an Editorial Committee presided over by Dr. Marcus Jastrow, the learned author of a Dictionary of the Talmud, as Editor-in-chief. As the work progressed, it became evident that the undertaking was more in the nature of a fresh attempt at translation than of a mere revision of a previous effort; accordingly, the Book of Psalms, which had been allotted to a member of the Editorial Committee, Dr. K. Kohler, was issued from the press in advance of the whole Bible. The small volume, neatly printed in a handy form, appeared in 1903. Dr. Jastrow, who had seen it through the press, died two months before its publication. In 1905 the Editorial Board was reorganized under the presidency of Dr. S. Schechter, formerly of Cambridge, England, and then head of the Jewish Theological Seminary of America in New York. It was found, however, that the method of carrying on the editing of the translations thus far submitted through consultation by correspondence was slow and ineffective. At length, in 1908, Dr. Cyrus Adler, representing the Jewish Publication

Society, and Dr. David Philipson, on behalf of the Central Conference of American Rabbis, which body had taken up a project of issuing the Revised Version of 1885 in a form suitable for the Synagogue, came to an agreement which provided for a new Editorial Board consisting of seven members, three to be chosen by the Conference and three by the Publication Society, while the seventh member who was to be agreeable to both bodies should be Editor-in-chief. The choice for the latter office fell upon the present writer, who, upon receiving his instructions from the Chairman of the Publication Committee of the Jewish Publication Society, gave his entire time to the work for a space of eleven months, from September 1, 1908, to August 1, 1909, during which period he prepared a manuscript draft of the new version. In addition to manuscripts prepared by the former Revision Committee, some of which had been revised by the old Editorial Committee and were accompanied by learned annotations chiefly from the pen of the late Dr. Jastrow, he had before him the two Anglican versions of 1611 and 1885, Leeser's work of 1853, other translations in various European languages done by Jews, and while he naturally surrounded himself with an apparatus including the best efforts, old and new, of biblical scholars, rejecting no help from whatever source it came, he made it his busi-

ness to consult at first hand the ancient versions
and the chief Jewish commentators of medieval and
modern times.   When in December 1908 he met his
colleagues on the Board (to which by appointment he
acted as Secretary) consisting of Drs. S. Schechter,
Cyrus Adler, and Joseph Jacobs, representing the
Publication Society, and Drs. K. Kohler, David
Philipson, and Samuel Schulman, representing the
Conference of Rabbis, he set forth to them the principles which had guided him in the preparation of the
draft, a transcript of which containing the Pentateuch had been forwarded to all of them in advance.
The principles were discussed and somewhat modi-
fied by the whole Board, the body electing Dr. Cyrus
Adler as its Chairman.   Through sixteen sessions,
each lasting ten days or more, from 1908-15, the
body of scholars worked in conference upon the draft
submitted to them.   The mode of procedure was as
follows: the propositions embodied in the manuscript draft, if unchallenged, were allowed to remain.
When challenged, a new proposal was made and, if
seconded, discussed.   A vote was then taken, and if
supported by majority, the proposal was entered.   In
the case of a tie, the Chairman had the casting vote.
The first proofs of the manuscript thus amended were
sent out to all the seven members of the Board.   The
result was a mass of annotations returned by the

Editors, infelicities of expression and imperfections of style being removed and good renderings excised that they might make room for better, and so many of them as were supported by a majority or could be disposed of by a general rule of the Board were immediately spread upon the proofs. There remained a small number, less than three hundred instances, which it was thought proper to reserve for discusssion in a final meeting, the seventeenth, which took place in the autumn of 1915. On this occasion likewise the vote of the majority prevailed, the Chairman again being given the casting vote in the case of a tie. Two members of the Board, Drs. Schechter and Jacobs, alas, died shortly after the final session. The task of seeing the work through the press fell to the surviving members, and no efforts were spared to guard against misprints and to insure typographical neatness. The cost of preparing the manuscript and of printing the first edition was borne by the Jewish Publication Society, which at an early stage had created a Bible Fund; the largest contribution amounting to $50,000 came from that noble patron of Jewish learning, Mr. Jacob H. Schiff. Not only was the gift ample to cover the expenses of the present undertaking, but a balance was left for an enterprise which was the chief concern of the late Dr. Schechter who constantly urged it upon his colleagues of the Publication Committee. It is the scheme of preparing a popular commentary on the Bible in the English language. The first-fruits of the Commentary plan, which naturally it will take a generation to carry to a finish, appeared in 1908 in the shape of a small volume containing the Book of Micah in English with an accompanying commentary.

The Merits of the New Translation. The present writer is too closely identified with the new Bible translation, which left the press in 1917, to express an opinion on its merits. It will not escape the fate of the two Anglican versions, and it will be the subject of criticism. If it will survive, superseding perchance Leeser's single-handed effort, its place in the estimation of the competent judges in the world of scholarship and in the affection of the hearts of the Jewish people in all lands where the English tongue is spoken by them will be due to whatever scholarly accuracy, simplicity of diction, and closeness to Jewish sentiment it may possess. Its salient feature, as the reader will gather from the Preface, consists in the happy blending of the double heritage which is the Jew's in the vast domains of the English Empire and in these United States. No translation in the English tongue, however, can be anything but a revision, a revision of the English Bible of 1611, itself a revision. All attempts at modernizing the Bible English must necessarily fail. Once and for all time the revisers of 1611 fixed the model for all future undertakings. Naturally the later revisions of the nineteenth century constituted a help which was gratefully made use of. In matters

The Jew and the Scriptures. of interpretation there was great room for improvement. The Jew, to whom the Scriptures were given, who treasured the sacred writings in the synagogues of the dispersion, in whose memory the meaning of the original largely, if not wholly, persisted, who, though at times he might be swerved into far-off fields of mental activity, was again and again recalled to the Book, may be trusted to have a truer and more adequate knowledge of it. A wanderer through the nations, he has spoken many tongues; for the unlettered he provided translations; but he never lost sight of the original, a minimum knowledge of which every Jew must possess, while the thorough interpretation was left to the care of the specialist. Whatever the progress of biblical learning has been, however thankfully the share of Christian workers in the vineyard of the Lord must be acknowledged, the verbal meaning of the Scriptures—and with that alone a translation is concerned—stands pretty much where the Jewish grammarians and commentators of the Middle Ages left it. ' Surely a poet is the poet's best interpreter, and a philosopher the philosopher's.   In the same manner it requires a religious mind to understand psalmist and prophet, and only he that is nurtured by Jewish thought, itself rooted in the Scriptures, may hope to master the scriptural Word in its fullest and deepest import.   Only a Jew can say on approaching Holy Writ: This is flesh of my flesh, and bone of my bones.   He must possess himself, it is true, of the philological method and the completest apparatus; but he alone can add thereto that which ensures fullest comprehension: the love for his own, for the thought that makes his innermost soul to throb, which still lives in him albeit faintly, so that his understanding of the Scriptures, mediated though it be by philological effort, becomes to a considerable extent indeed immediate, just as the language of the Scriptures is to him in a large measure a living tongue.'

CHAPTER VII

AGENCIES FOR CIRCULATING THE BIBLE

To make the Word of God understood by all those to whom the original was a sealed book was the aim of Bible translation. But all those efforts would have failed of their purpose had there not been pious souls who made it their business to render the work of

The Work of Distribution. distribution possible, that those that were not blessed with worldly goods might with the smallest outlay procure a copy of the Scriptures. It is a duty incumbent upon every Jew to transcribe the Torah or to have someone else transcribe it for his use. The copies used in the synagogue were habitually the gift of wealthy and generous individuals. Before the age of printing only the wealthy could afford the cost of having Bible manuscripts copied or of securing older manuscripts by purchase. Such copies constituted the heirlooms of families; and, as is the fate of all books, they frequently changed owners. ' Wealth and riches are in his house; and his merit endureth for ever '—this blessing the rabbis apply to him who causes copies of

8

the Scriptures to be made and then loans them to others. The Christian monasteries gave employment to their inmates through the multiplication of copies of the Scriptures; the costlier ones with their illuminations were works of art, and men, but particularly young women, who boasted of good penmanship, were much sought after. The emperor Constantine requested Eusebius, the bishop of Caesarea, to supply him with fifty copies of the Bible to be distributed among the principal churches of Constantinople. Don Samuel Gacon defrayed the expenses of the printing of the Faro Pentateuch (1487); the Ixar Pentateuch (1490) was made possible through the generosity of Solomon son of Maimon Salmati, and the Lisbon Pentateuch (1491) names a certain R. Eliezer as its noble Maecenas. The expense of issuing the revised French Geneva Bible (1588) was defrayed 'by certain wealthy men who sought no gain for themselves but only to serve God and His Church,' and that of producing the first Bible printed in America (Cambridge, 1663) was borne by the ' Corporation for the Promoting and Propagating of the Gospel of Jesus Christ in New England ' founded in 1649. The Port Royal version of the Gospels in French was issued in 1667 in many forms and sizes, including very cheap editions for the poor; we are told that pious persons ' sent out from Paris a great number of colporteurs to sell copies at cost price, or even less, and defrayed the expense by voluntary gifts.' In modern times societies were formed for the express purpose of circulating the Scriptures.

Societies for Circulating the Scriptures. The earliest was the Cannstein Bible Institute at Halle, founded in 1710, which passed at the founder's death to the care of the famous Orphanage, founded in the same city by Francke in 1698, and has issued some six million copies of the Scriptures. Far greater have been the achievements of the British and Foreign Bible Society, founded in 1804.

British and Foreign Bible Society. In the year of the tercentenary of the King James Bible (1911) it could pride itself upon having spent nearly sixteen millions sterling and issued more than two hundred and twenty-nine million copies of the Church Scriptures complete or in parts. Versions had been published in some five hundred languages or dialects.

American Bible Society. In America the earliest Bible Society was founded at Philadelphia in 1808. The American Bible Society was organized in 1816 in the city of New York, with Elias Boudinot as president. It has now a record of a century of achievement. One hundred and fifteen million Bibles have issued from its presses; its total budget for 1915-16 aggregates the sum of $652,300.

It has published translations in over a hundred languages.

To these two Bible Societies we are indebted for the cheap editions of the Bible in Hebrew. The large edition of the masoretic text by the late C. D. Ginsburg is being issued at the expense of the British

The Languages in which the Scriptures are read to-day. Bible Society. In England, an English Bible may be had for the price of tenpence and in this country for seventeen cents. Through the medium of the many versions, naturally for the most part based on the Anglican Church Bible, the Hebrew Scriptures, wholly or in part, have penetrated into the darkest nooks of the five continents, and have reached the farthest isles of the sea. In Europe, the Bible has been made accessible not only in the manifold dialects of the English language, but also in Irish, Manx, Gaelic—Welsh, Cornish, Breton (Celtic); in Icelandic, Norwegian, Swedish, Danish (Scandinavian); next to (High) German also in Dutch and Flemish; in the descendants of the Latin, Italian, French, Spanish, Portuguese, Romansch (in the valleys of the Upper Inn and Upper Rhine), Roumanian; in Modern Greek and in Albanian; next to the Church Slavonic, in Russian, Polish, Bohemian, Servian, Croatian, Slovak, Slovenian, Bulgarian; in the

Baltic languages, Lithuanian, Lettish, Wend; in Ossete (Central Caucasus). On both slopes of the Pyrenees the Scriptures are read in Basque; translations have been made into Finn, Esth, Lapp, Ziryen (government of Vologda, N. E. Russia), Hungarian (Finno-Ugrian stock); into Georgian (Caucasus); into Turkish. As we cross into Asia, we find the natives provided with the Scriptures in Armenian; in modern Persian, Balochi (in Baluchistan), Pashto (in Afghanistan); in Sanskrit, still the language of the learned all over India, and in the multitudinous dialects known as Indo-Aryan (Asami, Bengali, Gujarati, Hindi, Kashmiri, Marathi, Oriya, Pahari, Panjabi, Rajasthani, Sindhi, and on the island of Ceylon, Sinhalese); in the Munda dialects (Mundari, Santali) spoken in N. E. India; in the various Dravidian tongues (Kanarese, Khond, Malayalam, Malto, Tamil, Telugu, Toda, Tulu) in the provinces of India; in the Indo-Chinese languages (Burmese, Garo, Kachin, Karen, Khasi, Lepcha, Siamese, Shan, Talaing, Tibetan); in Chinese, Japanese (the Ainus in the northernmost islands of Japan, who speak a distinct language, read the Bible in their own vernacular), Korean, Mongolian; in the Malay dialects spoken in the Malay peninsula (Malay) and the adjacent islands, Sumatra (Batta, Nias), Java (Javanese, Sunda), Borneo (Dyak, Sihong), Celebes (Bugis,

Macassar). On the Australian continent and the islands of the Pacific Ocean the Scriptures are read in Ilocano and Tagalog (Philippine Islands), in Sangir (Sangir), in Mafur, Motu, Mukawa, Toaripi, Ubir, Wedau (New Guinea), in Mabuiag (around the Torres Straits), in Narrinyeri (South Australia), in Kusaie, Ponape, Ruk (Caroline Islands), in New Britain (Bismarck Archipelago), in Ebon (Marshall Islands), in Mota (Banks Islands), in Bugotu, Mwala, Ulawa, Vaturanga (Solomon Islands), in Aneityum, Aniwa, Eromanga, Fate, Futuna, Maewo, Malekula, Nguna, Opa, Raga, Santo, Tame (New Hebrides), in Lifu, Maré, Uvea (Loyalty Islands), in Maori (New Zealand), in Gilbert Islands, in Rotuma, in Fiji, in Samoa, in Tonga, in Tahiti (Society Islands). Coming back to Western Asia, we meet with Bible readers in Modern Syriac, Arabic, Mehri, Sokotri (Semitic); and as we cross to the continent of Africa, the Bible is read in another Semitic dialect, Amharic, in Abyssinia; in the Hamitic Galla in the same country; in the Berber Kabyli, in Northern Africa; then in a multitude of negroid and negro tongues: Swahili (on the eastern coast from Somaliland to Mozambique), Giryama, Gogo, Kamba, Shambala, Taveta (British and German E. Africa), Ganda, Nyoro (Uganda), Chewa, Tonga, Yao (on the shores of Lake Nyasa), Nyanja,

Thonga, Tonga (Portuguese E. Africa), Ndau, Shona (Rhodesia), Chuana, Pedi, Sheetswa, Suto, Xosa, Zulu (S. Africa), Nama, Herero, Ndonga (German W. Africa), Mbundu (Portuguese W. Africa), Benga, Bolengi, Fang, Fioti, Galwa, Kele, Kongo, Luba, Mongo, Mpongwe, Ngombe, Poto (in the Kongo states), Dualla, Isubu, Efik (Kamerun), Yoruba, Ibo, Nupé (Niger Territories), Ewe (Togoland in Dahomey), Hausa (Sudan), Accra, Ashanti (Gold Coast), Grebo (off Cape Palmas), Temne (Sierra Leone); on the island of Madagascar the Scriptures are read in Malagasy. For the benefit of the aboriginal tribes of the American continent there exist Bible translations in Acawoio, Arawak, Cherokee, Chippewa, Choctaw, Cree, Dakota, Eskimo, Lengua, Mapuche, Massachusetts, Micmac, Mohawk, Moskito, Muskoki, Nishga, Osage, Tukudh, Winnebago.

It is well to remember that a great many of these languages have become known only through Bible

Some of the Translators. translations, the preparation of which required an infinite patience born of the zeal of the missionary. Among the men (and women) who considered it as their blessed work to bring the Word of God within the reach of far-off tribes by means of translations in their native idioms we may single out William Carey,

' the Wycliffe of the East,' Joshua Marshman, Robert Morrison, Karl Friedrich August Gutzlaff, Henry Nott, John Williams, John Gibson Paton, Robert Moffat, George Leonard Pilkington, Canon Robinson, and Bishop Shereshewski, the ' Christian Jew.' Several other ' Christian Jews,' like Chwolson and Levinsohn in Russia, brought their ample learning to bear upon the delicate task of perfecting the translations which the Bible Societies undertook to circulate. The trials of a ' Bible Society agent ' have been described by George Henry Borrow (1803-1881) in a book ' glowing with freshness, picturesqueness and vivacity,' *The Bible in Spain* (1843). But the labors of translators, agents, and colporteurs were amply repaid by witnessing the effect which the Bible Word brought about everywhere. A notable instance may be cited. A Malagasy woman, Rafaravavy, went to purchase an idol. The maker had none ready, and asked her to wait while he made one. He thereupon went out into the forest, and cut down a small tree. Of the trunk he fashioned the idol, and kept the branches for fuel. When preparing the evening meal, he used some of these to boil his rice. The woman saw all that happened, and went home carrying her purchase. A day or two later a missionary read in her house some passages of the Scrip-

The Power of the Book.

tures, including the forty-fourth chapter of Isaiah.
' He heweth him down cedars, and taketh the ilex
and the oak . . . Then a man useth it for fuel; and
he taketh thereof, and warmeth himself; yea, he
kindleth it, and baketh bread . . . He burneth the
half thereof in the fire; with the half thereof he eateth
flesh; he roasteth roast, and is satisfied; yea, he
warmeth himself, and saith: " Aha, I am warm, I
have seen the fire "; and the residue thereof he
maketh a god, even his graven image; he falleth down
unto it and worshippeth, and prayeth unto it, and
saith: " Deliver me, for thou art my god." ' The
woman immediately forswore idolatry, and became a
devoted Christian. The words of the prophet in the
Hebrew Scriptures uttered thousands of years ago
approved themselves as potent to convert a far-off
African heathen.

The Jewish Publication Society of America has
for a quarter of a century assiduously and successfully labored in the field of encouraging
and propagating Jewish literature in the
English tongue. Its crowning achievement is undoubtedly the new English
version of the Hebrew Scriptures and
the projected Bible commentary in English. The initial steps in both undertakings have
been made possible chiefly by the generosity of the

The Task before the Jewish Publication Society.

noble American Jew who embodies the best traditions of his race, and whose name will be linked to all those pious men of the past who made the multiplication of Bible copies and prints possible. The Society will truly have completed its task only when it shall be placed in a position to print and distribute the copies of its version at a low cost, to the end that the poorest among us may have access, in the tongue which he and his children speak and love, to the Word of God which is the heritage of the congregation of Israel.

CHAPTER VIII

THE DIFFICULTIES INHERENT IN ALL BIBLE TRANSLATIONS

A frequent query must now be answered. ' Is not the Word of God one and the same? why then should Bible translations differ?' The common assumption is that with a working knowledge of the language of the original and a dictionary at hand the translation is easy. Yet translators habitually make apologies for

The Difficulties Confronting the Translator. their shortcomings and point out the difficulties with which they are confronted. ' The translator's preface' has a stereotyped content. Everywhere we meet with the same diffidence and anticipation of unfavorable criticism. The prototype of all prefaces to Bible translations, the Prologue to the Greek Sirach (chapter II), tersely expresses the difficulty when it observes that ' things originally uttered in Hebrew have not the same force in them, when they are translated into another tongue,' and the translator is quite certain that the same fault attaches to the Greek version of ' the law, and the prophets, and the rest of the books,' which preceded and guided his own effort. Likewise the rabbis in Palestine were very much troubled about the difficulty of adequately rendering the Torah into any language, though at times they conceded that it might be done into Greek. The peculiar delicacy of the translator's task is emphasized by the greatest masters of style, and interesting is the consensus of opinion that prose is more difficult to translate than poetry.

The dictionary meaning is far from exhausting the real meaning of a word. It is one thing to under-

Untranslatable Words.
stand a foreign text and quite another to translate it into the pure and idiomatic speech of free composition. At every turn we feel the cramping influence of foreign modes of expression, when ' pen and tongue are attracted by the language of the original.' Moreover, it is altogether an erroneous notion that words of one tongue are immediately convertible into words of another. We speak of coining words, but words are not coins of current value, that is, of uniform sense. The dictionary furnishes the general meaning; when we come to apply it to a specific instance we are thrown upon our own resources. Puns and plays on words can rarely be imitated, though the attempt was made in the Greek version (Judges 10. 4). Proper names are of course untranslatable. Cer-

tain familiar names in the Bible have passed into English in the form given them by the earliest Greek translators. We say Moses and not Mosheh; on the other hand we call his successor Joshua, though in Greek he became Jesus. The Greek translation of Chronicles-Ezra-Nehemiah known as I Esdras delights in tacking on Greek endings to Semitic names, and the historian Josephus goes farthest in this direction. On the other hand the literalist Aquila reproduces the proper names in their Hebrew form: Mose, Josua, Josiahu, &c. Two opposite tendencies were clearly operative in the dispersion and in Palestine.

The Appearance of Strangeness avoided. Weights, measures, and coins are as a rule taken over in their foreign nomenclature. Thus the English reader may for a moment be startled to learn that Solomon's molten sea contained two thousand *baths* (I Kings 7. 26). Yet at times the Authorized Version uses the general word 'measure' for the particular Hebrew measure in question (see for an example II Kings 7. 1). The Jewish Publication Society Version did the same in Zechariah 5. 5 ff. 'Pound,' in I Kings 1. 17, and elsewhere, sounds rather strange in Palestine, but not more so than the anachronistic 'diaphanous garments of Lacedaemonian make' in the Septuagint of Isaiah (3. 22). Where exactness is not requisite, translators seek to avoid the appearance of strangeness. The Scriptures, Oriental, Palestinian, Jewish in origin, have by the very agency of translation become a book for all peoples and places and times. In the vernacular the Bible must be adapted for men who are not concerned with the things that interest the student of antiquity.

It frequently happens that the translator, vainly seeking an equivalent for a Hebrew word or phrase,

Words and Conceptions Peculiar to certain Civilizations. realizes that translation deals not so much with words as with civilizations. Words are but sounds and symbols of things, and these things pass away with the civilization that produced them.

To transplant a definite civilization bounded by time, place, and race must needs mean a shifting and displacement and weakening of the original. Where the original speaks of hallowing a city to God, we say that it was destroyed; where the sacred writers refer to war as sanctified, we call it declared or prepared. Even contemporary cultures vary, and there is give and take in the business of word-making. The name travels with the thing, as for instance *kindergarten;* somehow we cannot translate *esprit* or *weltanschauung;* and French and German writers retain untranslated English terms like *sport* and *gentleman,* distinct products of the British civilization. Every Jew knows what is meant by *eshet hail;* a pure and pious and kind and charitable woman indeed, but also one that possesses power and ability, faithfully attending to her household duties, rising early and toiling all day long that her husband and children may have their comforts. But when in Proverbs 31. 10 the King James Bible denominates her a *virtuous* woman, the adjective is certainly too narrow in the modern sense of the word.

Due Regard to the Genius of the Language into which the Translation is made. Translations have been likened to the reverse-side of Dutch tapestries: the threads are the same, but so twisted as to produce almost a caricature. The translator finds himself face to face with the dilemma, how to combine fidelity to the original with due regard for the genius of his own language. Some languages, like the German, are pliable. French and English, on the other hand, are more rigid. Translation, according to Maimonides, is a species of original composition, and the translator a companion to the author. Bible translations of ancient and modern times run the whole gamut from the interlinear, which translates ' not words, but syllables,' to the free reproductions, which read more like commentaries than translations. Among the ancients, Theodotion, and in modern times the Anglican Version of 1611, may be singled out as avoiding the two extremes. The diction of the original is preserved; in every line the peculiar scriptural style reveals itself in all the simplicity of Hebrew prose, in all the grandeur of sacred poetry; not a word seems to be lost; yet frequently the Hebrew expression is recast, where a crude literalness would fail to produce on the English ear the effect of the original.

The right kind of a translation must not turn itself into a diffuse commentary, but an abbreviated commentary every translation must necessarily become.

The Uncertainty of the Sense. Where the original admits of more than one interpretation, the translator must choose one to the exclusion of the others. It is for this very reason that the rabbis frown upon all translations. With them the multiple sense of the scriptural word is an accepted fact. There is not a verse, they maintain, which may not be understood in two or three different manners, and the children in king David's time knew how to interpret the Torah according to forty-nine 'faces.' The rabbinical varieties probably refer to the legal deductions or moral lessons; nevertheless it could not have escaped them that the simple sense itself was a matter on which experts were divided. 'Any reader of the Bible in Hebrew,' so wrote Dr. Schechter, 'knows only too well how many passages there are that have been from time immemorial the despair of the commentators and have defied all their attempts at elucidation, and yet read smoothly enough in our versions. Take, for instance, the " Song of Deborah," or the sixty-eighth psalm, or innumerable passages in Job which are still the subject of controversy by scholars but which do not rouse the slightest suspicion in the man who relies upon his English Bible.' The poet Immanuel of Rome (about 1300) makes king David in heaven summon all the commentators of the Psalter, headed by David Kimhi, and their worth is to be tested by the staggering task of expounding the eighth and sixtieth psalm. Of the two concluding verses of the thirty-sixth chapter of Job commentators enumerate some thirty different explications. But the simplest passages in any book of the Bible are often a source of perplexity to the commentator and translator. The fourth verse of the sixth chapter of Deuteronomy, which under the name of the Shema' is repeated by every devout Jew twice daily and has been on the lips of dying Jews for centuries, has been rendered in half a dozen different ways. There are examples in the Bible where a deeper, more spiritual, or more widely applicable (universalistic) meaning has superseded the original sense in the consciousness of the Jewish people. ' The Bible is and was at all times a Word

9

full of fresh life, not a dead book belonging to a particular age and dependent for its meaning on the time
when it was written, but replete with new truths and
keeping pace with the national spirit as it impressed
its own stamp upon the sacred text ' (Geiger).

Points on which Christians and Jews Disagree. It is unavoidable, of course, that the
Scriptures which are held in veneration by
Jews and Christians should occasionally
become the battle-ground of the two relig-
ions. Fortunately with the greater number of instances the translator is not concerned at all, the Christian application to the life
and death of Jesus being a matter of interpretation
solely, while the wording is and remains neutral.
Such in particular is the case with the Servant's Tri-
umph through Martyrdom in Isaiah 52. 13-53. 12.
But a few passages there are on which the versions
of the Church and the translations of the Synagogue
must differ, and modern Christian commentators are
forced to acknowledge that the Jews are right. The
three most notable examples are found in Isaiah 7.
14; 9. 5; and Zechariah 12. 10. A further instance
might be afforded by Psalm 22. 16 (17), but there the
question turns about a disputed reading of the original. Jewish scholars of the type of Heidenheim are
free to confess that the uncertainty is of ancient
times antedating the schism which led to the rise of

Christianity; of a deliberate alteration from an anti-Christian motive there is not the least trace whatsoever.

A Christian scholar, recently pleading for a new edition of the received Hebrew text of the Scriptures, expressed his conviction that its makers did the very best they could with the material at their disposal.

The Text of the Original. Emendations. The fixing of the text coincided with the admission of a writing into the collection consigned to the keeping of the synagogue as Holy Writ. In the case of the Torah we have it on the authority of the rabbis that a model copy kept in the Temple court was the standard after which new transcripts were corrected and that there existed a guild of correctors in the pay of the Temple treasury. Other books, in particular those belonging to the third division (the Ketubim, or Writings), must have circulated privately, uncared for by the watchful official eye, and when they were transferred to the synagogue their text had suffered under the hands of careless copyists. When it is remembered how, for example, in the persecution under Antiochus Epiphaness the sacred scrolls were ruthlessly destroyed, the marvel is that the condition of the text is not much worse than it is. That the received text is in need of correction, or, as the technical term goes, emendation, is recognized by the medieval Jewish students of the Bible. None perhaps went so far as Ibn Janah and his admiring follower Tanhum of Jerusalem, who have frequently anticipated the suggestions now going by the name of modern emendations. In the nineteenth century, Krochmal and Luzzatto fearlessly emended the received text. The tendency among modern scholars, Jews and Christians, lightly to distrust the text of the Synagogue is discountenanced by more serious students. A judicious handling of the ancient versions often brings to light superior readings. But whether by the aid of the versions or by mere conjecture, the business of textual emendation requires a sure tact which few possess.

The translator is not called upon to re-write the original. A translation destined for the people can

The Translator's Exigencies. only follow the traditional text. Nevertheless a translator is not a transcriber. He must endeavor to make the Hebrew intelligible. He is therefore frequently forced to use circumlocution, to add a word or two, to alter the sequence of words, and so on. When he is confronted with a textual difficulty of the lighter order, he will, if he can, avoid the obscurity by deft manipulation and sometimes by the addition of a few words. Such are the translator's exigencies which have been faced by the ancient and modern versions frequently in the same manner. Where a

divergence occurs in the traditional text itself, as
between the reading in the body of the text (ketib)
and the alternate reading or correction on the margin
(kere), a Jewish translator must necessarily follow
the latter which has become authoritative in the Synagogue. There are cases in which the marginal reading is clearly the inferior, and sometimes both are
unacceptable. The traditional accents, marking stops
according to sense, are naturally a great help. Ibn
Ezra laid down the principle that no interpretation
running counter to the accents should be followed.
Yet he frequently enough sinned against them. Here
the translator, if he chooses to be a sinner, will find
himself in good company.

The margin in the King James Bible, retained with
modifications in the Revised Version, is really a remnant of the annotated editions. It serves
a fourfold purpose. It gives the literal
meaning of the Hebrew where in the
text, in obedience to the genius of the
English language, a freer rendering
has been adopted; alternate renderings implying a
different interpretation (sometimes the information
is added that the meaning of the Hebrew word or
phrase is obscure or unknown); references to divergent readings from Hebrew manuscripts or ' ancient
authorities '; and lastly, explanations without which
the purport immediately intelligible in Hebrew would

**The Margin
in the
Anglican
Versions.**

be lost in translation. The wise words on the subject found in the preface to the King James Bible have been quoted above (chapter V). A modern scholar maintains that there are four hundred words in the Hebrew Scriptures the meaning of which cannot be ascertained. Yet in none of the four aspects is the margin of the two Anglican versions exhaustive. Such matters must be left to the commentary; in a translation which has respect to the needs of the people they are bewildering. After all, to quote again from the preface to the Authorized Version, we must not 'weary the unlearned, who need not know so much; and trouble the learned, who know it already.'

It will have become clear to the reader by this time why it is that Bible translations do and must differ. **The Differences of Translations do not touch the Essentials.** The modern man will not find solace in the rabbinical doctrine of the multiple sense. There can be but one meaning to the word of law-giver, prophet, historian, psalmist, or teacher of wisdom; unless it be that here and there, of a set purpose, the sacred writer plays, as in riddle and parable, with the double meaning. But even there the business of the translator is to express the surface meaning, the proximate sense. The Bible, of course, is literature, and literature of a high order, which to be enjoyed requires utmost clarity in the most trifling particulars. But the Bible is first and foremost a religious book; it is read by the devout that they may be confirmed in their faith, and for that faith the Word of God as contained in the Scriptures, dealing as it does with the eternal verities of God and Providence and the destinies of His elect people—in this its larger meaning the Word of God is one and the same. According to the Jewish mystics, the heavenly Torah was written in black fire upon white fire; the Torah which was committed to the care of mortals must needs have been written in ink upon skins or parchment. The ink may have faded, and the parchment may have become brittle, but withal the fiery Word still speaks to us through letters and dots, and with unimpaired force the faith that was implanted in the heart of the Jew is translated to untold millions in the diverse tongues of humankind.

INDEX